EMPTY CHURCH

WHY PEOPLE DON'T COME & WHAT TO DO ABOUT IT?

BY
STANLEY E. GRANBERG

Copyright © 2022 Stanley E. Granberg

All rights reserved. No part of this publication may be reproduced, distributed, or transmitted in any form or by any means, including photocopying, recording, or other electronic or mechanical methods, without the prior written permission of the publisher, except in the case of brief quotations embodied in critical reviews and certain other noncommercial uses permitted by copyright law.

All Scripture quotations are taken from the *Holy Bible*, New Living Translation, copyright © 1996, 2004, 2015 by Tyndale House Foundation. Used by permission of Tyndale House Publishers, Carol Stream, IL 60188, All rights reserved.

ISBN: 978-1-957837-08-6

RECOMMENDATIONS

Empty Church is a book whose time has come—regrettably! Dr. Stan Granberg has not only been a keen observer of the church but is also an effective counselor and healer. *Empty Church* has great wisdom for churches that are struggling, as well as for healthy churches. What is occurring in our churches and in our culture demands a return to pure and simple Biblical faith, without all the accoutrements added in the 20th Century. For any Christian desiring your congregation to be healthy and to fulfill its Biblical mission, this book will be a blessing.

Mike E. O'Neal, JD
Chair, Heritage 21 Foundation
President Emeritus, Oklahoma Christian University

In *Empty Church*, Stan Granberg lays a foundation for understanding a few things that are crucial for church leaders in a time of shrinking churches. In rapid succession, Stan explains the cultural state of churches, the cultural state of our world, and the growing gap between them. This book will equip you to make sense of your church's situation and what options you can explore for the future. Stan has done a masterful job at being both prophet and pastor...challenger and comforter...as he guides us on a difficult journey to discover what is next for our churches.

Matt Dabbs
Editor, *Wineskins Magazine*, Wineskins.org

I enjoyed reading *Empty Church* immensely. Even though it is focused primarily on churches of 75 members or less, it is extremely relevant to my congregation of 500 or so. *Empty Church* is a compelling account of why so many churches are dying and how bold and godly leadership can create, with God's help, a more faithful and enduring community of faith. Granberg's assessment of the crisis most churches are facing is spot on. His language is clear, visionary, and engaging. His solutions are both doable and urgent. An essential book for Christians seeking to understand their predicament, revive their hope, and transform their future.

Jack Reese, PhD
Author of *At the Blue Hole: Elegy for a Church on the Edge*

This is a wonderfully comprehensive book and exactly what you will need in the new normal to lead a turnaround church. Everyone realizes we are facing a new reality: with skepticism on the rise and church attendance on the decline. I have found few books this comprehensive at addressing this reality as the book *Empty Church* by Stanley Granberg. If you want a book that covers all the bases, in a clear and concise way, and that all church attendees can understand - get this book. You need it. And, you will use it!

Bob Whitesel DMin PhD
Award-winning author and directional leader of the MissionalCoachesNetwork, ChurchLeadership.university and Leadership.church

Empty Church is a book written by a serious missiologist, great practitioner, and a leader with a shepherd's heart. In his current offering, Dr. Stanley Granberg takes us through a journey we are all watching, the emptying of the North American Church. His refresh data, practical steps, and reflective questions provide an excellent tool for the local church leadership to address the issue. Yet the best part of this book is the hopeful tone throughout its pages as the author challenges you to see your church from God's kingdom-building perspective.

Gary Rohrmayer
Author Spiritual Conversations
President Converge MidAmerica

Empty Church came at the perfect time for me and my ministry! Thanks Stan for shedding light on the changes that have been happening in churches across the country. More than that, *Empty Church* brings real, practical help

- biblical insights and strategies to help church leaders be faithful in times of great challenge. This is a book I want in the hands of every church leader where I serve.

Gordon Dabbs, PhD
Preaching Minister, Prestoncrest Church of Christ, Dallas, Texas

With the mind of a scholar (Open University Ph.D) and years of practical experience (church planter and leader), Stan Granberg adds value to the ministry of all who have a heart for helping churches navigate this uniquely challenging season. *Empty Church* is full of especially practical and well-researched observations and options for the future. Stan does not simply diagnose the difficulties, he realistically points church leaders to a range of solutions for their contexts. Most churches are prime for Revisioning, Renewal, Redevelopment or Repurposing. Stan and Heritage 21 are valuable kingdom partners for discerning next steps! I heartily recommend Stan Granberg's *Empty Church!*

Dr. Doug Peters
Interim Ministry Partners

Stan Granberg is a church leaders' friend. And real friends always tell you the truth—like it or not. It's no secret that the American church is experiencing empty pews. More than the pandemic, cultural winds and tides have been shifting for decades against the Christian faith. The church has some choices to make and in these pages, you'll be given choices. *Empty Church* is not theory, rather it provides practical tools grounded in the mission of God. With the heart of a missionary, the tools of a church planter, and the analysis of a researcher Granberg systematically shares help and hope for your church.

Grady D. King, DMin
Leader: HOPE Network

Sometimes faithfulness looks like the strength and speed of a sprinter; at other times it's more like the steady endurance of the marathoner. But, sometimes in church life, faithfulness looks like the handing of a baton. That is an act of trust—trust in others, but more importantly in God. In this book, Granberg—from his decades of experience in mission work, church planting, and working with church leaders—helps churches who may be at that point."

Mike Cope
Director of Ministry Outreach, Pepperdine University

WARNING: This book will irritate you! With characteristic clarity, challenge, and compassion, Stan outlines where the church - specifically your church - needs to own its failures and let go of sacred cows from the past. That's no easy thing! Packed full of stats, tools, self-assessments, and tactics, Stan gives strategy and direction to reshape your church into a revitalized and effective disciple-making community that reaches the lost for Christ. If leaders and churches properly engage with these resources, it will be like receiving a personal consultation from Stan!

Alex Absalom
Dandelion Resourcing

Stan Granberg has devoted his life to planting churches in Kenya and North America and to coaching church leaders. In this wonderful resource, he provides three things that every church leader needs: a realistic assessment of our current situation, hope that is rooted in God's power and ongoing work, and concrete steps for moving forward. Whether your church is thriving, about to close, or somewhere in-between, this guide will help church leaders envision the future and take next steps.

Mark Powell
Dean, Harding School of Theology

Stan Granberg's book, *Empty Church*, is truly outstanding. In brief form, he has insightfully outlined the challenges facing today's church and has offered a practical way forward. I will enthusiastically recommend this book both to small churches discerning their future and to larger churches who want to have a greater impact.

Jimmy Adcox
Minister, Southwest Church of Christ, Jonesboro, Arkansas

Stan is a wise guide after all of his years of ministry, coaching and teaching. I recommend this book, especially the emphasis on disciple making.

Bobby Harrington
CEO – Renew.org and Discipleship.org

Contents

BEGINNINGS	18
PART 1: THINGS HAVE CHANGED	20
CHAPTER 1 – WHY IS IT SO HARD?	22
Family Around Here	23
Generational Core	24
Blood, Sweat, and Tears	24
Summarizing	25
Reflection Questions	26
Scripture Study	26
CHAPTER 2 – WHAT'S CHANGED?	28
Rise of Skepticism	29
Denial of Objective Reality	30
Mistrust of Authority	30
Results	31
Reflection Questions	34
Scripture Study	34
CHAPTER 3 – UNDERSTANDING SOME FACTS	36
Transformational Change	36
A Typical Congregation	37
Churches of Christ	40
Other Historical Churches	42
Transformational Power	43
Reflection Questions	44
Scripture Study	44

PART 2: ASSESSING YOUR CHURCH	46
CHAPTER 4 – THE LIFE CYCLE OF CHURCHES	48
Four Revitalization Options	51
Do This Now	54
Reflection Questions	54
Scripture Study	54
CHAPTER 5 – HOW IS MY CHURCH REALLY DOING?	56
The Quick 50	56
15 Questions	57
By the Numbers	59
Decision: Redevelop or Repurpose?	62
Conclusion	65
Reflection Questions	65
Scripture Study	65
CHAPTER 6 – LEADER RESPONSES	66
Not on my watch	67
But where will people go to church?	67
We got it right	68
We don't need help	69
We have plenty of time	70
Conclusion	71
Reflection Questions	71
Scripture Study	71
PART 3: REDEVELOPMENT	73
CHAPTER 7 - EVANGELIZING	76
Do You Believe It?	77

Everyone Is On A Spiritual Journey 80

The Journey to Belief 82

3 Question Conversation 83

5 Bucket Spiritual Diagnosis 85

The "My Spiritual Journey" Napkin 88

How Will Evangelism Impact Your Church? 91

How Do I Help My Church Become Evangelistically Active? 93

Reflection Questions 93

Scripture Study 94

CHAPTER 8 - SERVING 96

Service and Servant Evangelism 96

Three Steps to Servant Evangelism Impact 99

Reflection Questions 101

Scripture Study 102

CHAPTER 9 - DISCIPLING 104

The Mission of Discipling 104

Leading for Discipleship 105

How People Mature 106

House Churches, Discipleship Groups and Missional Communities. 109

Reflection Questions 113

Scripture Study 113

PART 4 – CLOSING WELL 115

CHAPTER 10 – CREATE AN ESTATE PLAN 116

What is Estate Planning? 116

Elements of Church Estate Planning 117

Challenges to Healthy Church Estate Planning 120

  Reflection Questions 121

  Scripture Study 122

 CHAPTER 11 – TIMELINE AND ESSENTIAL MARKERS 124

  Create Your Plan 125

  Default to Design 126

  Internal to External 129

  Growth Engine 133

  Identify Your Essential Measures 136

  Conclusion 138

  Reflection Questions 138

  Scripture Study 138

 CHAPTER 12 – WHAT IF IT DOESN'T HAPPEN? 140

  Set Your Priorities 140

  Deal with Real Estate Realities 142

  Management Challenges 142

  Celebrate Your Church's Life 143

  Reflection Questions 143

  Scripture Study 143

BIBLIOGRAPHY 145

ABOUT THE AUTHOR 149

FOREWORD

Let me tip you off on one of the most arresting insights in this important book: churches have life cycles very similar to human beings. The human life cycle is often 70 to 100 years; and the life cycle of churches often falls in the same range. Both move through seasons of steady growth, vigor, reproduction, effectiveness, stability, maturity, and eventually reduced capacity. Both humans and churches face the reality and challenges of aging and ending. But unlike humans, churches have the possibility—though it is somewhat unusual—of reversing the aging process and revitalizing their mission.

Empty Church proposes and outlines a strategy or game plan for renewing a church that is in steady, even serious, decline. The proposal is elemental—reduced to the bottom-line basics—and bold in its call. Seeking to reverse the church aging process, which involves calling the core members to some new and usually disorienting steps, takes faith and an adventuresome spirit. It takes energy and sustained commitment.

Here's another key insight from *Empty Church*: "Connecting new people to your church is the only remedy for decline." Connecting new people will require what is called transformational or adaptive change. This kind of change means more than making adjustments or tweaking some things. It means big change. It means breaking with some deeply established and comfortable ways. It means taking some new steps. It is hard and often troublesome work.

Transformational change is built on experimentation, done wisely (we hope). But even done wisely "experimental innovations trigger resistance—*internal resistance. . .* ," says Todd Bolsinger. "Systems seek to secure the status quo, to experience and maintain equilibrium. Families, companies, organizations, and congregations are wired for homeostasis. The emotional processes, ways of relating and being, decision making, symbols, values and other parts of the organizational culture naturally work together to *keep things the same*."[1]

So it's a bold and steady challenge. And Stan recognizes that this kind of change is required to connect new people and reverse the declining trajectory of a congregation. Both the profound changes occurring in North American culture and the dynamics of the natural aging of a congregation make it so.

Taking up the challenge of transformational change calls for mission-focused leaders willing to push against the natural resistance to change. To choose and embrace a pathway of transformational or adaptive change is a bold move. Some aging churches will be called to that. However, others, after prayer and discernment, will choose to care for their small flock without disrupting the long-established pattern of their life together—an honorable choice. In this case responsible leadership will plan carefully for the aging and ending processes, including an estate plan. This book serves as a very realistic and practical guide to making these choices.

Churches in the West are experiencing a great shaking in this season. It's not only the challenges brought by the COVID-19 pandemic; it's that we face the mounting pressures of a post-Christian Western culture. These sharply rising cultural pressures in North America are forcing churches to re-examine their mission. The church in the West is being dislodged from its mostly comfortable setting in a so-called "Christian America." That situation had its great virtues and great flaws. But it is gone. We are finding ourselves in a situation somewhat similar to Christians in the first three centuries, before the rise of Christendom. The early Christians did not enjoy cultural favor; indeed they occupied the margins of their culture and regularly found themselves odd outsiders, sometimes scorned, sometimes persecuted. They maintained a strong sense of being "resident aliens," diaspora communities. But through these fraught early centuries the church grew steadily.

Like those churches, we now find ourselves in a missionary situation in our own culture. Amid decline and uncertainty, we are being forced to ask ourselves: Can we learn to think like missionaries in our own towns and

---

[1] Todd Bolsinger, *Canoeing the Mountains: Christian Leadership in Uncharted Territory* (2018), 127.

cities? Can we shift from being churches that send missionaries to being missional congregations in our own places? That's a big question facing declining congregations.

Stan is a seasoned and trusted guide in helping churches understand and respond to such questions. For years, he has been analyzing congregations, training church planters, coaching church leaders, studying the literature of mission, and guiding congregations through renewal processes and—sometimes—repurposing processes. He has provided vital wisdom and actionable steps for aging churches.

So as you are deciding if this guidebook is what you need, consider these additional questions addressed in the pages ahead:

- Why is leading a church more challenging today than in earlier times?
- How can we discern where our church is in its life cycle?
- What is the difference between "redeveloping" and "repurposing" our church?
- What specific steps can we take to connect more people from our community to our church?
- How can we begin to think differently about evangelism in this new time?
- What are the key factors in making the decision to close a congregation?
- What are the basic elements of an "estate plan" for our church's future?
- How can we celebrate the life of our aging congregation?

If these questions interest you, this is the book for you.

Leonard Allen

Dean of the College of Bible, Lipscomb University

BEGINNINGS

How is my church doing? That's the question many church leaders are asking. Pre Covid-19, many churches were in a place where they were wondering about their future, expecting things to be fine, but trying to understand why it seems so much harder to keep the church functioning than ten or twenty years ago. Now, with the Corona pandemic, it feels like the future is even more uncertain!

Since 2005, I've had the opportunity to visit with hundreds of congregations of the Churches of Christ across our nation. Our fellowship of Churches of Christ is widespread, and our congregations are numerous. In fact, until 2000, our fellowship was in the top ten list of largest Christian affiliations in the United States. We've slipped down to about #15 now.

I've met with church leaders in the typically smaller, "exodus movement" churches in the Northeast, where our fellowship is sparsely represented; the large churches of the South who need traffic police to safely empty the parking lot; the homegrown, independent churches of the Midwest; and the transplanted Oklahoma/Texas churches typical of the west coast from California to Washington.

Of the almost 12,000 congregations of Churches of Christ reported in *Churches of Christ in the United States 2018* (Royster), here is what a typical congregation is like:

- Our congregations are typically smaller as far as the number of people attending worship. Most of our churches are under 100 in attendance, usually hovering around the 60-person mark. This gives them a strong "nuclear family" feel.

- Congregations are led primarily through men's meetings that occur irregularly according to need or through a small eldership of two or three men. Regrettably, too often, their main tasks are to keep people happy and keep issues to a minimum.

- There may be a partially supported minister at that 60-person mark. If the church is closer to the 100-person mark, the minister will be the only full-time employee with either a part-time or volunteer secretary. If there are multiple staff, it is typically the minister and an administrative secretary. Other needs are met by volunteers who take on leadership tasks as necessary to keep the church operating.

- Our congregations are mostly traditional in their practices, following what became the norms for the Churches of Christ through the 1950s and 1960s. They still try to meet Sunday mornings and Sunday evenings with a Wednesday mid-week Bible study.

Empty Church is written with churches in mind that are in this majority in our fellowship, but any church looking for ways to engage the next quarter-century will find good tools and starting points here. While my personal church fellowship of Churches of Christ is in focus, most denominational or community churches will find help here too.

PART 1: THINGS HAVE CHANGED

How do you lose 1,178 churches? That's a lot of churches, and that's how many our fellowship of Churches of Christ lost in the last thirty years. Let's say that each of those churches averaged 100 people, that's 117,800 people. The fact is, in those same thirty years, attendance at Churches of Christ dropped 185,606 people. In 1990, *Churches of Christ in the United States* reported 1,280,178 people meeting in 13,092 churches. In 2020, our reported numbers were 1,094,572 people in 11,914 congregations.

What has happened to your church since 1990? For many churches, thirty years ago, things were pretty good. The 1980s were growth years for many churches. So, by 1990, auditoriums were full and new education wings were hopping with excited children. Plans were often made for new auditoriums that would double the seating capacity so everyone could meet at the same time. Those were good years.

Since 1980 a seismic, some would say cataclysmic, cultural shift has occurred in America. I'm in my mid-sixties. When I was growing up, the church seemed to be a staple of American life. Almost everyone I knew had some church connection, at least by name. Today, that is no longer the case. Here are some numbers published reported by Greg Smith of the Pew Research Center describing religious activity in America in 2019:

- More Americans say they attend a few religious services a year (54%) than attend at least monthly (45%).
- Only 1 in 3 millennials attend religious services at least once a month. 22% say they never attend religious services.
- 29% of Americans say they never go to church (Statista).
- 26% of Americans claim no religious affiliation (down from 17% in 2009).

The Pew researchers summed up their study with this:

. . . the U.S. is steadily becoming less Christian and less religiously observant as the share of adults who are not religious grows . . . In other words, the nation's overall rate of religious attendance is declining not

because Christians are attending church less often, but rather because there are now fewer Christians as a share of the population.

The result of these religious shifts in the people around us also influences the people whom churches have counted on as members. Research by the Generis capital campaigns group demonstrates how the American cultural-religious shift impacts church attendance among committed Christians. In 2000, committed Christians attended religious services on average 3.2 times per month. By 2017, that had dropped to 1.8 times per month. (Gallaty and Swain, *Replicate*, 2020, p. 25).

The impact on churches is huge. If a church was averaging one hundred attendees in 2000, in 2017 they would average fifty-five. In the Covid world, George Barna reports that one-third of practicing Christians will not return to church. Now that church of one hundred in 2000 might have forty people attending in 2021. The church that was viable in 2000 is no longer viable in 2021. As a result, David Kinnaman (Terry Mattingly blog) predicted that one in five churches would close by the end of 2021.

Yes, things have changed. In Part 1, we will look more deeply at what has changed and why sustaining a healthy church is so much more difficult today than it used to be.

CHAPTER 1 – WHY IS IT SO HARD?

The church I consider my home church, the church that most formed my Christian faith, is the Lakeview Church of Christ in Tacoma, Washington. When my family moved to Tacoma in 1966, the Lakeview congregation was meeting in a small auditorium that could comfortably seat one hundred people. Classroom space was limited, and the fellowship was close. I saw that church grow. First, we added classrooms. Then the church bought a big piece of property on the downhill side of the original building. About the time I headed to Harding University in 1974, an architect, a teacher from a university back east, moved out for two years with his family to design a new worship facility that would reflect the Pacific Northwest character.

Those were great years. The church grew from a house church to an established church of eighty, and finally to one of the leading churches in the Pacific Northwest with over four hundred people gathering in two worship services. In my teen years, we never had a youth minister, but my teen experience was outstanding. The ministry staff was typically the preacher and secretary, yet the church grew and thrived. The church was nestled in the shadow of two major military bases—Fort Lewis Army Post and McChord Air Force Base—which meant the church had a constant stream of transferees. Yet there was a core of families that raised their children together, shared life, and formed a powerful center of influence for the Lakeview church. I can't imagine a better church for shaping my life and growing my faith. I grew up in the golden age of my home church.

Every church that has been around for any length of time has its own golden age, that time when people look back with the sense of, "That was a great time." Some churches are fortunate enough to have multiple "golden year" seasons as different generations of people take on the central roles that give churches life.

One of the first realities I notice when I work with an aging church is how difficult it is for their remnant members to recognize that their church has aged with them. Every church will face that point when their golden years are behind them. We'll see later how that passing occurs and what it looks like. But right now, let's look at three reasons why it is so hard to comprehend lifecycle changes in a church.

Family Around Here

My home church had a favorite song they have sung for close to fifty years. It's Bill Gaither's song, written in 1970, titled *Family of God*. I'm sure we started singing it as soon as it made its way onto the record label. The line our church loved and sang with gusto, standing in a circle around the auditorium holding hands, was, *you'll notice we say brother and sister around here. It's because we're a family and each one is so dear*. We sang this at baptisms, when new members were recognized, and sometimes just because we were together! It was our song.

That's what happens in good churches. People become family. They live life together. They invite friends and visitors to share Sunday lunches with them in their homes. They raise their children together, go to school performances and athletic events, and junior spelling bees together. They vacation together, sitting on beaches, hiking in the mountain, or just sitting around a campfire sharing a good smoke (fire-wise). People who are part of good churches love each other. They love to be together. They care for one another with meals and prayer and fellowship. They take meals to families when someone is in the hospital or homesick. They celebrate each other's birthdays and anniversaries, graduations, and weddings. They grieve when one of their numbers passes, and a family member is gone.

Such a rich, full-body life is the way it should be. Good churches gather people together into a faith family that supports discipleship across the lifetime of the believers. But "family" style body life also has dangers. It can produce a preoccupation for the members inside the church so strong that the "not yet" believers outside are forgotten. A family-style church can create an unintentional barrier for new people trying to get in. There is so much life identity that gathers around member relationships that they have no more social space to let new people into their group. Finally, members have seen and shared so much of life it is just hard for them to accept that one day their church may come to an end. There is a fog of memory that makes it hard for people to see the aging of their church. While being "family around here" is a great positive, it is also a bit of a two-edged sword.

Generational Core

A second reason church leaders may fail to see the reality of an aging church is that churches tend to be generational in nature. As I've worked with and studied churches at various times in their life cycle, I've noticed that there is a generational core that forms the heart of every church. This core creates the energy, sees God's vision, and provides the willpower to see that vision happen.

This generational core typically forms around younger families who are in their child-bearing and rearing years. In my home church, the innermost core was half a dozen or so families. These men formed the first eldership, and most remained as elders for years. These families were the energy core. They were the dependable workers around whom others gathered, grew, and contributed in their own way.

This generational core also gives identity to the church. They are the tone-setters. It's sometimes hard to admit, but the personal experiences, the personal theological perspectives, and even the personal preferences of this generational core form the way the church looks, feels, and acts. While there is a downside to this personal influence on the character of the church, I love the way Will Mancini (*Church Unique*, 2008) recognizes this as the way every church is formed uniquely for God's purposes for that time and place and people. Mancini gives us a way to celebrate the unique contributions of each church because of its generational core.

Eventually, that generational core of people ages, and unless they are replaced by a new core, the church will sink into decline.

Blood, Sweat, and Tears

The last reason we'll consider as to why it is so hard for churches to recognize their reality of aging is that those who were the builders, the generational core, don't want to see their investment disappear.

It takes a tremendous amount of work and sacrifice to grow a church. When Luke records the church planter Paul's words to the early church, *"They encouraged them to continue in the faith, reminding them that we must suffer many hardships to enter the Kingdom of God"* (Acts 14:22), he wasn't just speaking metaphorically. Ask our new generation of church planters about this. These pioneering ministers will say that planting a new church is the most difficult ministry they ever pursued. Fortunately, most of them also say planting a church may be the most rewarding ministry experience as well. Growing a church is hard business.

It is the generational core of a church that gives the blood, sweat, and tears required for a church to grow, thrive, and experience its golden years. These are amazingly self-sacrificing people. When my home church was in those early growth years, I remember working weekends and nights pouring concrete, mudding drywall, painting, and sweeping, all the while laughing and enjoying the company of others at labor for the Lord.

This generational core also contains the dependable financial givers for the church. Not only can the church count on these consistent givers week by week and month by month, but these people will also lead the way in special contributions, making significant, life stretching financial commitments to extend the ministry of their church. You may remember people selling houses and cars, giving up vacations (for three years!), and selling their jewelry to give towards a church building project. Their sacrificial lives provide the example that trains those around them in giving. Significant discipleship training occurs around special project giving which spreads out from the core to envelope the whole of the church.

People who have sacrificed so much to see God's kingdom advance through their church don't want to see that sacrifice lost, even if it was made thirty or fifty years ago. To them, it is "their" yesterday.

Summarizing

In this chapter, we surveyed three reasons church leaders struggle to accept the aging of their church:

1) Family around here

2) Generational core

3) Blood, sweat, and tears

The result of these three realities is they turn us around backward. A church planting friend of mine, Roger Gibson, often said that many churches try to walk towards the future backward! All they can see is their nostalgic past, the way things used to be. That's when we hear statements like, "Our problem is we've gotten away from the basics," or "It was really great when we were doing . . ."

Sometimes the golden age of our past is the very thing preventing us from entering the glorious future God could take us to.

Reflection Questions

1. Which of the three reasons given above have you experienced that makes it hard for people to comprehend your church is aging?

2. When was the golden age of your church?

3. What was it like?

Scripture Study

Acts 14:1-23

- What does this passage say about God?

- What does it tell us about people?

- What does it say about the kingdom of God?

- How might the believers in Iconium, Lystra, and Derbe have considered these years their golden years?

CHAPTER 2 – WHAT'S CHANGED?

My thirty-something-year-old son is a pretty savvy tech guy. He seems to be able to grasp today's technology and make it work. I, on the other hand, find I need a handy third-grader around to change my clocks, work my streaming services, and keep my phone up to date. I hate it when I go to bed and my phone looks one way, but when I turn it on the next morning it's changed! My son continues to assure me, "Change is always good, dad." I don't think I believe him yet.

We are living at a time when life is moving at a warp speed. Eric Schmidt (M.G. Siegler, 2010) CEO of Google, stated in 2010 that every two years we are creating as much new information as we did from the beginning of history until 2003! I don't know how true that statement is, or if I can even wrap my mind around it. However, it does confirm that the world we once knew no longer exists. Every year is truly a brave new world. This is why church leaders cannot lead their churches to the future backward. We've got to turn around and go forwards!

Why is this world so different now? I don't know if you kept up with the discussion that hit the general academic world about 2000. The terms modernity and post-modernity were hot topics. I was teaching at Cascade College at the time. The philosophical discussions in the college world about what defined post-modernity seemed like a never-ending debate. But my experience with students absolutely verified one significant fact: the millennial students (those born between 1981 and 1996) were different from those that came before them. The Millennials were our first generation fully formed in the post-modern era.

The reason this is important for you is that if your church began sometime between 1950 and 1980 (as most U.S. congregations were), your church is rooted in the modern era. The things that your church did, the way you did them, the reasons you did them were all rooted in a specific way of thinking that doesn't exist among millennials or those generations following them.

This generational shift may be the most significant reason why it's so hard for churches planted in the 20th century to make the changes necessary to thrive in the 21st century. Let's look at three of these most significant generational shifts.

Rise of Skepticism

To understand the millennials, we need to start with ourselves. I'm assuming, like me, you were born sometime between 1940 and 1970. Give or take a few years, that puts you into the midst of the Boomer Generation, the largest and most influential generation of the 20th century.

Boomers have a distinct view of the world that goes by the term "modernism." We view the world as a stable, rational entity that runs according to observable, consistent laws. Our quest is *"to bring rational management to life in order to improve human existence through technology* (Grenz, *A Primer on Postmodernism*, 1996)." Unpacking Grenz's statement, we believe there is an objective reality, "out there," that anyone with a good mind can observe and know. Knowledge is definite, objective, good, and makes sense. With enough effort, rational thought, and good intentions we can make the future better than the past.

Millennials and those that follow them don't see the world as having an objective reality or a universal code of morality. They are not convinced that life will always get better, that the world is a safe and secure place, and that science and technology will meet all our challenges. In fact, they're often downright skeptical about anything that smacks of certainty or makes universal claims—like Christianity.

Think about what the Millennials have experienced. They have now lived through a Great Recession and a global pandemic. Financially, they may never achieve what their parents did. They live with instant technological gratification that is supposed to connect everyone better than ever before, yet they are one of the most socially isolated, awkward, and anxious generations in history. They can't even trust the world itself any longer as global warning looms over them like an impending biological catastrophe. Who wouldn't be skeptical?

Denial of Objective Reality

The second major change is that the 21st-century generations don't see a universal, all-encompassing reality—a universal truth. Reality is what the individual makes of it. Why not? We never even thought of the idea of "fake news" until recently. In the post-modern world, it is the perspective of the individual that carries weight. Consensus is gained as individuals share ideas with their peers. Those ideas get passed around and around until a general "truth" (a consensus) forms. That truth does not have to be consistent. It does not have to be testable. It does not have to be logical. What truth does have to be is relevant.

One area where this denial of objective reality is creating stress is the issue of sex and gender identity. For most of history, sexual identity was a binary question, a person was either male or female, and people were born that way. But for many today, gender is viewed on a spectrum, a sliding scale, where a person can choose where they want to be on the spectrum, almost at will.

To a modern mind, these conversations are disturbing. To the post-modern mind, they are essential. To those of us who understand the Bible as God's Word to us as His people, it is doubly concerning. God himself is "above." He is the way, the truth, and the life (John 14:6).

Mistrust of Authority

Finally, the 21st-century generations distrust authority, particularly any kind of authority that appears inherited (like male-based leadership). This mistrust of authority is expressed against political leaders, news media, social institutions, and religion. The Deloitte Global Millennial (Tomáš Roba, 2020) survey says that 26% of Millennials and 24% of Gen Z have zero trust in business leaders, while the rate is 27% and 30% for traditional media, 45% versus 41% for political leaders, and 45% and 49% for religious leaders It's understandable to see this mistrust. Today, no one can do or say anything publicly (and sometimes privately) that is not likely to be recorded. The more information available, the more obvious it is when promises are failed to be kept.

But when millennials are asked about this mistrust of authority, they see a difference between what they perceive as institutional and personal authority. One blogging millennial (Lifeway, "Authority," 2022) said it this way, "Millennials don't disrespect authority (some do, sure, but as a whole); we disrespect authoritarianism. What I mean by this is that Millennials value direction, leadership, and authority that is based on know-how and experience. But we resist the type of authority that originates in a 'because I said so' attitude." In general, millennials resist positional authority, but they are open to relational authority—an influence that is gained through a genuine relationship.

Results

I want to assure church leaders if you find that leading a church today is more challenging than it was earlier, you are 100% correct. These fundamental shifts have changed the spiritual market in which our churches compete with the world—and it is not easier. While the powers of darkness have always been adversarial to God's kingdom of light, I have not experienced another time where the attacks have been so consistent and have come from so many directions.

Here are some of the results of the rise of skepticism that every church in America is wrestling with:

Rise of the Nones
The category "None" comes from the U.S. census collection that provides "none" as a category for religious affiliation. The "None" designation has become a shorthand way to refer to people for whom religious affiliation is not important. In the 1990 census, only 8% of Americans checked the "None" box. In the 2020 census, over one-third (Michael Lipka. 2020) of those in the US census identified themselves as having no religious affiliation. These people may not be atheists or even antagonistic towards church and Christianity. James Emory White calls them "apatheists" (*Rise of the Nones*, 2014). Nones consider organized religion irrelevant to their life.

The impact on churches is that these folks don't go to church anymore. Many Nones came from families that did go to church—at least some. I've called these people 3-G people. Their grandparents were faithful members of a traditional Christian group. Their parents were affiliated but didn't make church involvement a priority. And for the 3-G people, the church has never been part of their life.

Many church leaders I know have lived this out. I hear it this way: "I raised my kids here in this church. They were married here. But now I can't seem to get them to be interested. I just wish my kids and grandkids would come to church with us." I hate to break the news to them, but I do. Their kids and grandkids will most likely not find a place in their parents' or grandparents' churches. The best thing the older generations can do is to take a spiritual journey with their kids and grandkids. This means asking questions and offering a listening ear. It can also provide the opportunity for the older generation to express why their church life has been so meaningful to them. Engaging in the dialog that allows open sharing of perspectives is important.

Peeling Away Cultural Christians
In some parts of the US, in the southern and midwestern states particularly, Christianity has been an ingrained part of life. If a person wanted to be a respected business leader, a city or state official, association with a church was essential. These people were believers. They generally lived a good life. But Christianity was sometimes just skin deep. These church attenders have been designated as cultural Christians, people who went to church for reasons of politics, business, or acceptance. In other words, they wanted to be culturally accepted.

Today, the social pressures that kept these cultural Christians in church no longer exist. With the pressure off, cultural Christians are disengaging from their traditional churches. We see this reflected in the rate of attendance. In the 1990s, faithful, committed Christians attended church, on average, three times a week. Today, the typical committed Christian may attend religious services only once or twice a month. If your church averaged 300 attendees on a Sunday in 1990, it is likely that pre-Covid you were averaging somewhere around 125.

Two-Decision Conversions
The first people I baptized were a couple of young men following the Rolling Stones tour up the west coast in their VW van. They came to our church asking if we baptized by immersion and would we baptize them. I

did. These two men represent the one-step conversion process most people had in the last century. Today, most people go through a two-step conversion.

I was returning to Portland, Oregon from a consult with a church in Texas that was trying to raise their level of evangelism. I noticed in the waiting area that most passengers on my flight were women. In fact, on the row, I sat, and the rows in front and behind me, I was the only man. As the flight began, I introduced myself to the two women beside me. They were hospital administrators flying home from a national conference. As the conversation continued these two women eventually asked me what I did, and the shoe dropped as I told them, "I train pastors to plant new churches." At that point, the woman next to me turned to her traveling companion and said, "I can't believe we're sitting next to a Christian." Then she asked me, "Are you one of those evangelical Christians?" When I answered probably so, she turned again to her companion and said, "Oh my God, who do we have to be sitting next to him!"

What this woman expressed is an increasingly commonly held assumption: Christians are bad, and churches are worse. Years ago, Christianity was considered good. Churches were seen as valuable presences in their communities. That's no longer the case in more and more communities.

Today, most people who become Christians go through a two-step conversion process. Their first decision is to consider whether Christianity could ever be something good enough to investigate. Their second decision is whether to become a follower of Jesus. My experience is that this spiritual decision-making process takes, on average, from eighteen months to two years. Most churches are simply not prepared for people to take two years to decide whether they will become Jesus's followers. For churches that are small and declining, such a long cycle for evangelism is too slow to make a difference in their revival.

The landscape of Christianity in America has changed drastically in our lifetime. Christianity has been displaced from its position as a cultural center and now sits at the edge of an increasingly disinterested culture. People we used to depend on for consistency and growth aren't there anymore. It is harder and takes longer to walk with people towards a decision about Jesus.

When we began this chapter, I said it is harder to grow and have a healthy church today than it was twenty or thirty years ago. I hope this doesn't discourage you; I do hope it gives you a better sense of the challenges that your church faces today.

Reflection Questions

1. Which one of the three fundamental shifts described in this chapter do you feel the most?

2. Have you personally encountered someone who feels Christians are bad? What did you learn from them?

3. How does the idea of a two-decision conversion shift your expectations of sharing the gospel?

Scripture Study

Romans 1:16-32

- What parallels do you see between the world as Paul described it and today?

- Where can you see God's mercy in this?

- How does the gospel show its power today?

CHAPTER 3 – UNDERSTANDING SOME FACTS

We've talked about the changes around us and why leading a church is so much more difficult today than it was in the last century. Every time I use the phrase "last century," it reminds me that what we're facing is 100% real! Most churches in America were planted in the last century. They were intended to serve and designed to thrive in the world of the last century—and they did! The challenge we're facing today is that what worked in the last century is not likely to work this century.

The changes we have experienced in our technology, economy, and society are so radical that it changes the way we must view change. As preachers, elders, and leaders of God's congregations we are faced with a paradigm shift, a change of perspective so far-reaching it requires us to rethink and rebuild the way we do "church."

Transformational Change

We call this kind of paradigm shift *transformational* change. The kind of change most of us have practiced is *incremental* change. Incremental change challenges us to do things better, but they're the same things we've been doing. It's like a new year's resolution that we're going to lose some weight, exercise more, take more days off, or whatever. Our resolution is to do those things better, more effectively, so that we reach our goal. Incremental change in a church is sprucing up the building, making services run smoother, or hiring a new, younger minister. Incremental change can be described as 10% change. We become better—by 10%.

The cultural shift between the 20th and 21st centuries is of such great magnitude that incremental change is ineffective. We've got to engage in transformational change. Transformational change is radical. Where an incremental change requires us to do the same things better or more efficiently, transformational change requires us to do different things. We must learn to think about challenges in new ways and become adventuresome in seeking options. Transformational change is not measured by the percentage of change, it's a "10x" magnitude of change. This is what makes transformational change so scary; we move from the known to the unknown, from the familiar to the unfamiliar. We must quit reading the maps of our past that tie us to what we know and learn how to navigate towards what is yet to be.

I want to give you a strong caveat here, or maybe a way forward. Not every church can, or should, work for transformational change. People choose to be part of a church because it fits them. They like that church the way it is. To impose the kind of transformational change it takes to renew a church for extended life in this new century means changing the church so much it would no longer be the church for them.

Sometimes the best option for church leaders is to keep serving the people who are in their church as best they can in the ways that make the best sense for those people. That is an honorable choice. But with that choice, you need to recognize that your church will have a limited lifespan. That might be another two, five, or even ten or fifteen additional years, but there will be an end. What you should do is make a plan now about when and how you will bring your church to a close. We'll spend time on that process later in the book. For now, your primary decision is whether your church should pursue transformational change for renewal or to serve your church well until it is time for it to close.

You might be asking yourself three questions about now: 1) Do we really need transformational change? 2) How should we attempt transformational change? 3) What should we expect if we don't change? Let's look at these three questions.

A Typical Congregation

First, let's start with what a typical congregation among Churches of Christ looks and feels like to 21st century people. I want to do this by describing an experience I had that represents a very typical church situation.

I was asked by a church in Texas (where everything is bigger and better—right!), to do a weekend assessment with them. They knew that the world had shifted underneath them, and they wanted to see what they could do to fix things. Their only minister and six elders were willing to spend most of two days investigating their situation.

As my wife and I drove to the church we noticed the neighborhood was a lower economic property with a high multi-racial mix. Driving into the church's parking lot we were met by a brick building built in the 1960s with the main entrance tucked under a low, overhung drive-through. As a first-time visitor, driving through a huge, empty parking lot, what we saw was a factory-like building with no signs of life—and in fact, no signs at all. There was nothing warm, inviting, or indicating much life or activity was happening here. The feeling was this place is closed.

As we toured the building, everything spoke of age, old age. The carpet, the walls, the décor—even the smell—all said, "I'm from the 1970s." The children's wing was no longer being used, except for a small meeting hall where a Hispanic congregation of about thirty-five people met.

When we walked into the auditorium it smelled bad, like an old basement where the carpet had mildewed. The auditorium was built to hold 400. The back rows were roped off to move their group of 125 towards the front to be closer together. They were proud of their "newly" renovated bathrooms with orange Formica countertops, yellow painted walls, and sheet vinyl on the floor.

Their worship services were traditional, consistent with our fellowship. They sang from songbooks stored in the back of the pews, though they did project the *Paperless Hymnal* (not necessarily a positive). The solo song leader selects songs from a repertoire of golden oldie standbys, like *Blessed Assurance, I Need Thee Every Hour,* and *When I Survey the Wondrous Cross*. The preacher and their public presenters wear suits and ties for services. The church membership is decidedly older, although there were a few families with children.

Most of the members, and all the elders, had raised their families in that church. They had wonderful memories they shared together of days gone by. They told us of this church's rich history, beginning in 1964. At one time they had over 400 people meeting together. They had planted at least one thriving church in the new area of the city in the 1970s. Most of the history they shared with us was from what they did before 1990. They couldn't come up with anything that stood out to them in this century.

They shared with us their discouragement at how their Vacation Bible School and some other after-school activities to attract families had not attracted any new neighborhood people. In fact, their church represented a "donut church," where the church is in the middle of a big hole, while its members live in a large ring around it. The members, including all the leaders, had moved twenty to forty-five minutes away as the immediate neighborhood around the church dropped down the economic scale.

Financially, the church is distressed. At one time they had three full-time ministers on staff. Now they can only afford the one pulpit minister, whom they are hoping to keep until he retires. The building is so large and requires so much updating that they feel overwhelmed about doing much with it.

Here is a church with a great history, but it has become old. Its facilities are worn out, and so are its leaders. Their membership has been on a steady downward trend for over twenty years and their neighborhood has changed around them so much they have few connections to their neighbors. This is a classic mid-20th century church trying to find life in the 21st century.

I felt one of their elders described their emotional condition best in a private, side conversation he had with me. He pulled me away at a break, and with tears in his eyes told me, "My children were born, raised, and married in our church. They love our church, but they won't come here. My daughter told me just the other day, 'Dad, you know I love your church, but it isn't a church for us. We will never come back.'"

What do you think the future of this church will be? Will incremental change, like updating the bathrooms, help them? If you were guiding them, what would you tell them about their future? Hang tight to the end? Go back to the things they used to do? Hire a young minister and hope he attracts younger families? All these options are available. But the reality is, without transformational change that turns this into a church that looks, feels, smells, and acts as a 21st-century church, 21st-century people will not go there.

Now, let's shift from the micro look at this one proto-typical congregation to what is happening in the Churches of Christ as a nationwide fellowship.

Churches of Christ

Churches of Christ hit our numeric high-water mark about 1990. At that time, we reported 1,284,056 members in 13,027 congregations. If you're a seasoned leader you probably remember the 1980s. This was the time that many churches were at their largest or approaching their largest size. Larger churches, particularly in the south, were building big buildings to house their activities. Mission work was booming around the world. National workshops and university lectureships were drawing crowds of thousands. Those were good years for us.

I spent most of the 1980s in the mission field of Kenya. We left when the tide was high and so were our expectations for the future. When we left for Kenya in 1983, our sponsoring church was one of the early mega-churches in our fellowship, with over 1,200 attenders on a Sunday. When we returned from Kenya in 1993, that church had disbanded and sold its thousand-seat auditorium. The few remaining members met in a small house church. The rest had scattered into other congregations in the region.

The most recent statistics, gathered by 21st Century Christian (2020), reported that we now have 1,113,362 members meeting in 11,914 congregations. Here's what our fellowships' growth/decline trajectory looks like since 1980, as reported by *The Christian Chronicle* (Bobby Ross, 2012):

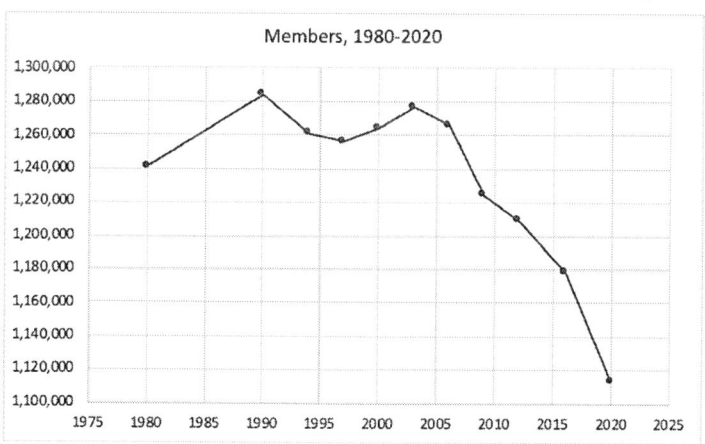

GRAPH 1. TRAJECTORY OF CHURCHES OF CHRIST 1980-2020

In 2020, Tim Woodroof and I projected a possible the future for the Churches of Christ. While any "crystal ball" gazing is risky, we looked at potential trends based on 1) our last thirty years of decline, 2) the aging of our current members, 3) our seeming lack of evangelistic activity, 4) the loss of younger generations to our existing churches, 5) our failure to plant new churches, and 6) the constriction on leadership and innovation produced by our elder-dominated leadership model.

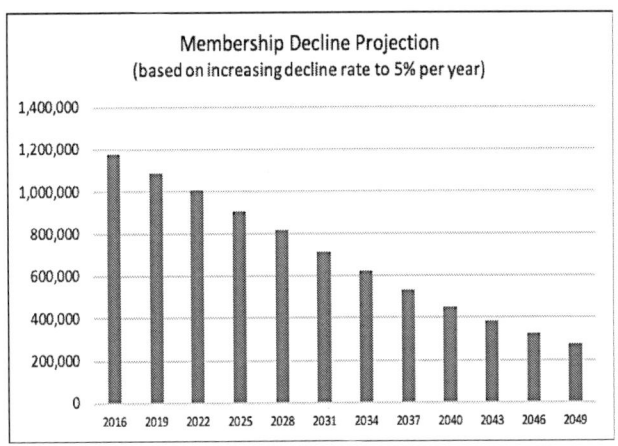

GRAPH 2: PROJECTED MEMBERSHIP DECLINE, 2020 - 2034.

If the rate of membership decline increases gradually over the next fifteen years (to 2034)—from 5% every three years to 5% annually—and remains at that level until 2050, the membership of Churches of Christ would drop from 1,177,783 in 2016 to just over 250,000 members in 2050. (See Graph 2.) That is an 80% loss! While this is a drastic extrapolation, it follows the pattern of evangelical congregational decline in attendance reported by the Hartford Institute for Religious Research (Yonat Shimron, 2021) in 2020, and that study was done before the Covid pandemic.

For congregations, the picture is equally grim. Smaller, older congregations will be disproportionally affected by declining membership trends, accelerated by Covid. These churches have older memberships and fewer resources to support ministers, ministries, and facilities. What will prove a struggle for churches over two hundred members will be devastating for many of the 55% of our congregations that average fifty people or less in attendance each week. As these mini churches lose what little critical mass remains, as current leaders and committed givers die, and the burden of maintaining aging facilities becomes overwhelming, smaller congregations will close at a more rapid rate. If the rate of congregational closings increases gradually (from the present rate of one hundred congregations a year to three hundred per year by 2034), and remains at that level until 2050, the number of Church of Christ congregations would drop from 12,237 in 2016 to about 2,800 in 2050.

Other Historical Churches

These numbers are so overwhelming they seem unbelievable. Surely it could not happen to us! But history does not support such optimism. Once a tipping point of decline sets in, the ability of a movement to sustain itself economically, socially, and to make new disciples decreases. Church membership plummets. The Wesleyan Methodist and Anglican churches—which once claimed large percentages of Great Britain's national population—are today only a fraction of their former size and in danger of extinction as culturally relevant movements (John Hayward, "Revival or Extinction?," 2002).

Traditional, mainline churches in America (includes the American Baptist Churches USA, the Christian Church/Disciples of Christ, the United Church of Christ, the Episcopal Church, the Evangelical Lutheran Church in America, the United Methodist Church, and the Presbyterian Church) accounted for more than 30% of American church-goers in 1975. That number fell to 11% in 2018 (Ed Stetzer, 2017).

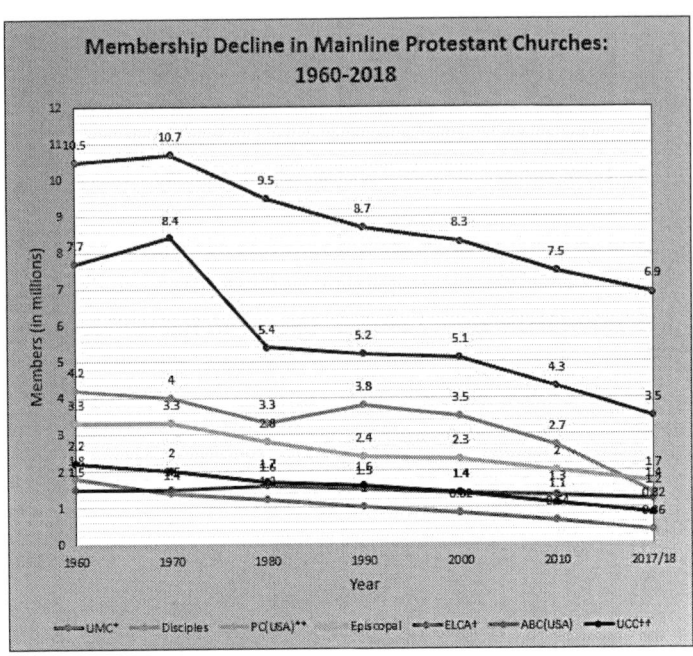

GRAPH 3. DECLINE OF MAINLINE PROTESTANT CHURCHES, 1960-2018.

Graph 3 shows what these churches' decline trends were from 1960 to 2018. Ed Stetzer (2017), prominent researcher of the American church says, "If the data continues along with the same pattern, mainline Protestants have an expiration date when [their] trend lines cross zero in 2039. . . they have 23 Easters left." It would be inaccurate to interpret Stetzer's statement to mean that by 2039 no more of these churches will exist. What he is saying is that their relevance will be negligible and their capacity to influence will be minimal.

Transformational Power

There are only two "powers" capable of effecting the sort of transformational change we talked about at the beginning of this chapter.

The first transformational power is the power of God. God does work miracles. As the Lord of resurrection, he has the power to turn this movement around and breathe new life into dry bones. We should—all of us—be in prayer for God's Holy Spirit to fall with fresh fire on ourselves and our congregations. But it would be foolish of us to keep doing the same things in the same way while expecting God to change the results. I believe God can intervene, but we must be willing to respond to his guiding.

The second transformational power involves the power of godly, bold leadership—fearless, mission-focused, kingdom-minded leaders—who dare take the purposes of God seriously and risk challenging the natural resistance of churches to change. We need leaders who are willing to make bold decisions. These leaders need to look beyond their own, individual congregations to see the bigger kingdom picture and be willing to resource God's kingdom work.

Are there such leaders in our churches, ready to beckon our members towards a different future? Yes. Will our churches naturally call these leaders forth and invite them to lead transformative change? Not necessarily, it's not natural. But God will do the calling and these leaders must be willing to listen—and act. I pray that you are this kind of leader.

Reflection Questions

1. Describe in your words the difference between incremental and transformational change.

2. What do you expect Churches of Christ will look like in 2050?

3. Are there any kinds of transformational changes you feel your church would need to make to be healthy and ready for a new future?

4. How do you feel about supporting transformational change to avoid your congregation continuing a negative growth trend?

Scripture Study

1 Peter 1:3-12

- When Peter speaks of an inheritance that is imperishable, undefiled, and unfading (1:4), how might we reconcile these words with the idea of transformational change?

- How might we understand Peter's description of encountering trials that test the genuineness of faith (1:6-7)? Does Peter mean staying the course until the end or is there another way to understand the idea of change?

- Peter ends this section in 1:12 speaking about serving those who will follow us. How might your church of today serve a church of the future?

PART 2: ASSESSING YOUR CHURCH

70% of people are *fact oriented*, they want to know the realities. Facts give perspective on what we're facing as church leaders. Here's a few critical facts you can share with your fellow church leaders and members:

- There are approximately 380,000 churches in America. This number has fluctuated a bit over the last twenty years, but 380,000 is a good number to remember.
- About half of these churches were planted before 1950, that's seventy years ago! I'll tell you why this is so important in just a bit.
- 70% of these 380,000 churches have fewer than one hundred people in attendance at their worship gatherings.

Here's what all these numbers may mean for you. If your church is a typical church in America, your church was planted about seventy years ago and you have less than one hundred people attending your Sunday worship event. This puts you in a precarious position as a church. It means your church is older, your members are older, and you don't have the extra energy or resources to absorb loss or to use to gain momentum. If you as a leader are feeling tired, worn-out, or just plain out of ideas, it's probably because these numbers we've just shared are working against you.

In Part 1 we looked at how things have changed and why that makes keeping a church healthy and growing is more difficult today than it was. In Part 2 we'll look at how to assess the current state of your church's health and status using a series of assessment tools.

While the assessment tools are relatively simple and easy to use, the willingness to accept reality is often much more difficult. Many times, church leaders are simply too optimistic about their church or emotionally unable to admit to their reality. Unfortunately, if one cannot gain proper perspective on their current reality, it is very difficult to make plans that will move the church forward to a better future.

I encourage you to first work through these assessment tools yourself. Give yourself time to reflect on them until you feel you are truly understanding your reality. Then, share these tools with your fellow church leaders, asking them to do the same. Once you have done this, then it will be time to come together to share insights and perspectives.

CHAPTER 4 – THE LIFE CYCLE OF CHURCHES

People have a natural lifespan somewhere around seventy to eighty years. What has amazed me is that research shows that generally churches have a similar life span, about seventy to eighty years, the same as people. But, where a living organism has a linear, progressive lifecycle that moves from a beginning to an ultimate end, organizations are able to revitalize, to circle back to renew or redevelop themselves. Churches have an organizational quality to them that gives them the opportunity to step backward in the lifecycle and extend their life or let them reform for a new life.

I use the following simple diagram to illustrate a church lifecycle (Figure 1). This bell curve represents the beginning of a church at the bottom left and the closing of that church on the bottom right. As a church goes through life it will pass through stages. Different church researchers and authors use different labels and a different number of stages. We're using a simplified approach that has just four stages to it. Let's look at these stages.

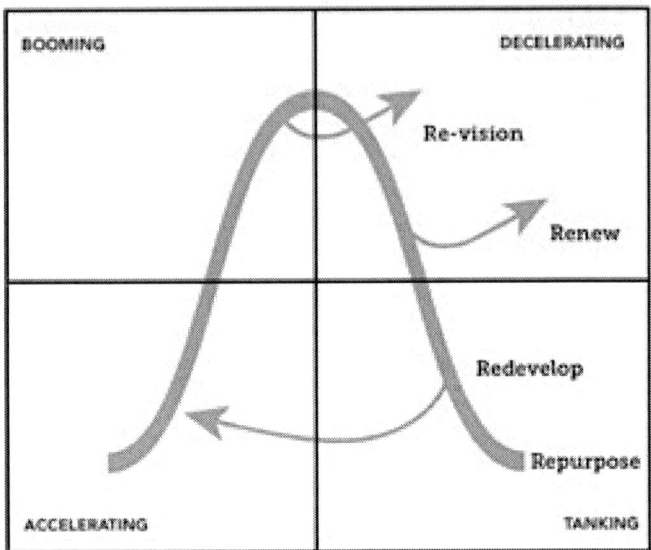

FIGURE 1. LIFECYCLE OF CHURCHES.

First, in the lower left quadrant, is **Accelerating**. This is where churches begin. New churches may launch from scratch, they may borrow people from a nearby parent church, or an older church may intentionally restart with a new name, new leadership and often a new location. New churches tend to have a clear sense of purpose and their goal is to gain enough new people to grow from formation to survivable. This happens in the Acceleration stage.

Next, in the upper left quadrant is **Booming**. If the new church does well, if it's able to attract and retain new members and its core activities are working, it will enter the Booming stage; it will thrive. Often, as the church ages, this is the stage people will remember and talk of as the "golden years" of the church. This is when the church is full of people; it's active and vibrant. It's the time when young families raise their children together and form bonds of love, loyalty, and appreciation.

These two stages, Accelerating and Booming, are where most of the growth in a church's life will happen. A church usually takes the first fifteen to twenty years of its life to grow through the Accelerating into the Booming stage. Churches often stay at the top of the curve for another fifteen or twenty years.

As a church ages and moves to the right, it enters the **Decelerating** stage. Early in this stage things still feel like they are going well. In fact, the early stages of decelerating may feel like the best it's ever been. The church is stable. It has a good core of consistent families who have been there for years. The leaders are seasoned and know each other well. The church probably has land, a nice building and money enough to support a variety of church programs and needs. But what sneaks up as time goes by is this central core of the church begins to age. Their children grow up, marry, and move away. The activities that were once signature events of the church are not as productive as they once were. People begin to wonder what's happening and there's often a cry to, "return to the things we used to do!" For the twenty to forty years of this stage, the growth of the church plateaus and slowly begins to decline, then the decline becomes more rapid as the church moves towards the fourth and final stage: Tanking.

Tanking is not a very kind word, but it is quite descriptive. At this point the church is typically fifty, sixty or seventy years old. Its membership is declining, new people may visit, but they don't stick around; resources of people, time and money are scarce. The faithful few feel more and more burdened as they try to meet all the needs of the programs and activities they used to do, but with fewer people and resources. The building now looks worn as regular maintenance and replacement of carpets and paint, lighting and bathrooms are no longer affordable. Eventually, the preacher leaves or retires to a part-time role; guest speakers are brought in to conduct the Sunday worship. At this point, the church is on life support, awaiting either a miraculous healing or the burial of enough of the few remaining people until they can't make it any longer. At this point, the building often is so old and worn it has little financial value, or it's been mortgaged, and the resources spent to sustain the dwindling few.

I encourage you to go to our website, Heritage21.org, create your account and sign up for our free video course *About Your Church's Future*. Here you will find six short video courses that will visually guide you through major considerations for your church. Video #3 is *Understanding Your Church's Lifecycle*. Not only will the video walk you through this material, you can take the free assessment to identify where your church is on the lifecycle curve.

Four Revitalization Options

At the beginning of this chapter, I stated that organizations have opportunity to reinvent themselves, to get a restart that moves them back up the lifecycle and extends their healthy lifespan. To go along with the four stages of the lifecycle, there are four revitalization options available for churches.

It's important to note that each of these options must occur at a specific point in the lifecycle. This timing is crucial. If you wait too long to accomplish a particular option you can't go back and say, "we're going to choose to do this one." You can only work with the option available at your current stage in the lifecycle. You cannot choose an option from earlier in the lifecycle.

Option 1: Revision – Revision occurs in the top two quadrants of the lifecycle. Revisioning requires the church to be healthy, with active leadership and the people and financial resources to make things happen. Revision consists of a complete review and updating of the mission, vision, and strategy of the church. Because of the speed of change of today's society, church leaders should lead their churches through a revisioning process every three to five years.

Unless you have an exceptional senior minister or leadership team, your best option is to bring in an expert from the outside to guide you through your revision process. The revision process I use is called StratOp, short for Strategic Operations. StratOp begins with a three-day creation weekend where I teach you to use tools and processes I've been trained in. This creation weekend is followed by a year of coaching to help you make the progress you've planned out during your creation weekend. There are other people and ministries who have their own assessment approaches as well.

The most effective point for revisioning is on the Booming side of the lifecycle, when energy, resources, and people are abundant. Revision on the Decelerating side is possible, but more difficult, as resources thin and energy diminishes. Revision is an option only when a church is reasonably healthy and has a good resource base of people, energy, and finances to draw upon.

Option 2: Renewal – Once the church drops deeply into the Decelerating stage of the lifecycle, the options become more difficult as resources, energy, and momentum drop to critically low levels. In the renewal option, the church must seek a path to reverse its decline, become attractive to new people, and find a new mission and vision that breathes new life into the church.

Renewal may be the most difficult option for a church because it requires the current members to change their focus from themselves to those who are not yet part of their church. I call this the shift from *Maintenance to Missional*. However, the church is at its current state because of what its members expect—and like. What got them to this point in the lifecycle is what will keep them there. In fact, Thom Rainer's research shows that only five percent of churches that try are able to successfully navigate a Renewal process.

Option 3: Redevelop – Once a church drops into the Tanking zone there are two final options available to them. Option 3 is to Redevelop. Redevelopment requires the church to have the will to transform itself into a new church. Redevelopment is starting a new church. To redevelop, the existing church will need to think and act like a new church. One church in California sold their building and used a portion of the proceeds to buy two units in a commercial property which they renovated to meet their needs as a sixty-member church. They have done well for a number of years in their new format. A church in a southern state sold their building, changed their name, and began meeting as a new church in a local school. Most of their members and leaders made this transition into the new church and have stayed with that congregation. Another church on the west coast did something similar, but most of their previous members dispersed into other established congregations. Only a handful joined with the minister to begin the new congregation. What is consistent with these churches that chose to redevelop is that they intentionally began again as a new church.

Our partners at Kairos Church Planting offer training that will walk your church through the redevelopment process with other church leaders who are working on their projects or plans for new churches.

Option 4: Repurpose – The final option is to Repurpose. If one of the previous three options is not appropriate or cannot be successfully implemented, the final option is to close the church and repurpose its "capital of faith" for good kingdom work. Repurposing is a very deliberate decision that allows the Tanking church to manage its closing process, repurpose its resources to help God's kingdom somewhere else, and to celebrate a life well lived. The Heritage 21 Foundation provides a pathway to close well, offering the technical skills to legally implement the closing decision and make the desired distribution of church assets your church wishes.

What makes the Repurposing option difficult is there are ALWAYS one or two people among the few remaining members who either can't see the need or won't allow the church to close. It takes an unselfish attitude for a church to decide it really is not doing much for the kingdom other than keeping house for their own happiness. It requires selfless hearts to see that the best use of the resources the church has stored in its lands and building is to sell them so they can be repurposed to help new churches start elsewhere and support good mission works that expand God's kingdom.

It's hard to say, but personal selfishness is the number one reason that churches that need to close decide not to close until they have no other choice. These churches live on life support, often using rental income to stay in their property. They hire preachers to come do their preaching and song leading for them for a few dollars a week. Their members feel satisfied that they are still meeting, but they have no measurable kingdom impact. Their only purpose is to meet until the last of them have died—or someone has taken their property from them.

I pray that if your church is in the Tanking zone that you will have the courage to accept that fact. You don't need to close the church immediately, but you do need to make the plans that will help you begin your transition while being good stewards of the kingdom resources God has given you.

Do This Now

Go to, Heritage21.org, create your account and sign up for our free video course *About Your Church's Future*. Video #3 is *Understanding Your Church's Lifecycle*. Complete your free assessment to identify where your church is on the lifecycle curve.

Reflection Questions

1. How would you explain the four parts of the church lifecycle to another church leader?
2. Has you church ever done a strategic revision?
3. Which of the four revitalization options do you feel is most appropriate for your church? Why?

Scripture Study

2 Timothy 4:1-18

- How do we remain faithful even in difficult times?
- What are the signs a church has "fought the good fight and finished the course?"
- What would it mean for a church to finish it's race well?

CHAPTER 5 – HOW IS MY CHURCH REALLY DOING?

Now we're at the point where it's time to take a deep breath and prepare to look at your church's reality. This will be hard work. Even leaders of healthy, active churches find it challenging to face their realities, recognize their weaknesses, and be willing to address what absolutely needs to be addressed today so they can have a better tomorrow. Leaders who are feeling distressed and uncertain about their church often find the search for reality even more difficult. But remember the axiom, if you don't find the bear first the bear will certainly find you.

Almost every church leader we meet with says they want to Redevelop or Renew their church when we ask them what they want to do. But what you may want to do and what you are capable of doing may be two different things. Thom Rainer, church growth researcher for the Southern Baptist Convention, says from his research and experience that only five percent of churches that are significantly down the decline slope or in the tanking zone of the church lifecycle are able to successfully renew or redevelop to become a healthy, growing church again.

Remember, your goal is to not beat yourself up. Your goal is to know what you face so you can face it well. That is the most God-honoring thing you can do. Anything less or anything else becomes Cain's sacrifice. So, let's get at it.

In this chapter I will lead you through a series of activities that will help you gain perspective about the state of your church and give you good clues as to the next steps you should consider most.

The Quick 50

First, let's do a quick assessment. Think of this as the quick 50 assessment. There are just three questions that use the number 50:

1. Is your church over 50 years old as a church?
2. Does your regular Sunday worship attendance run under 50 attendees?

3. Are your attendees mostly older than 50?

If you answer yes to all three of these questions, your church is in critical condition. This means your church will struggle to do much more than maintain itself—at least until a key member or two move or pass away and then even maintaining will be a struggle.

If your church is in this condition, it does not mean you have failed or are doing something wrong. It does mean your church is nearing the end of its lifecycle. Your job as a leader right now is 1) to care for your remaining members for your closing season, 2) set out a timeline for closing, and 3) make an estate plan that uses the property God may have blessed you with to bless new churches and other good works. If you take the next six to twenty-four months to do this, you will have done an excellent work.

15 Questions

This next tool asks you fifteen questions about your church. These questions will help you assess your current abilities and capacities for your future.

Instructions: Circle **Yes, No or ?** for each question.

1. **Yes No ?** We have updated Articles of Incorporation and By-Laws to protect our church legally.

2. **Yes No ?** Our By-Laws have a clear process for making decisions about the future stewardship of the congregational assets.

3. **Yes No ?** We have a history of navigating well times of important transitions.

4. **Yes No ?** We do not have any deferred maintenance items (roof, flooring, painting, parking, etc.) we cannot afford to repair or update within the next 12 months.

5. **Yes No ?** Our facilities are clean, well-cared for and attractive for ourselves and our guests.

6. **Yes No ?** We have significantly updated at least one of the following in the past five years: AV technology, worship stage, children's ministry area, auditorium lighting, bathrooms.

7. **Yes No ?** At our current level of giving, we are able to meet all our operating, facilities, and ministry staff obligations from our regular contribution.

8. **Yes No ?** We have 8 or more family units whom we are confident will give consistently and generously during a transition season.

9. **Yes No ?** We can operate at our current level of expenses without using saved or rental resources.

10. **Yes No ?** We have made significant changes in our worship experience in the last 5 years.

11. **Yes No ?** Our children's ministry is dynamic and well-operated.

12. **Yes No ?** We do not have unresolved issues (relational, doctrinal or otherwise) causing tension among our congregational membership.

13. **Yes No ?** We have at least one full-time staff person under 50 years old who has a prominent public role.

14. **Yes No ?** Our church leaders are physically, emotionally, and spiritually capable and energized for a season of transition work.

15. **Yes No ?** Our members are willing to follow the lead and decisions of our leaders.

Interpreting: Count your numbers of yeses. Here's how you can assess your score:

- **12 or more yeses.** Your church is in pretty good shape. Using a stop light analogy, you're in the green. You have been paying attention to your business and should have the abilities and resources to plan for your next season of church life. It is time for a season of strategic planning to guide your next few years of church ministry.

- **9 to 11 yeses.** Your church is in condition yellow. You are feeling the struggle for resources and people. You probably are asking yourself questions about what is wrong or why things aren't happening like they need to. This is your time to take immediate action. You should ask for help from outside resources who can bring knowledge and experience to help you plan a way forward.

- **8 or fewer yeses**. Your church is in condition red. You are in a danger zone. You need to take a very realistic look at your church, which includes the option of closing sometime in the next few years. Again, look for guidance from some outside resources. Heritage 21 can guide you to a church counselor from your region, probably someone you already know, who can help you think through your situation and make next step plans.

By the Numbers

While numbers never tell the full story, there are some numbers that are too important to ignore. I've found two sets of numbers important for understanding the condition of the church. The first are hard numbers. These are objective items, easy to count. The second are soft numbers. Soft numbers are more subjective and personal, but still important.

Hard Numbers

Instructions: For the hard numbers below, you may need to do a little research. These numbers will give you a snapshot of where your church is right now and nudge you towards a look to the future.

	5 Years Ago	**This Year**	**Next Year (estimate)**
1. Worship Attendance			
2. Baptisms			
3. Weekly Contribution			
4. Per Head Contribution			

In general, you want to see what trends may be happening at your church. Specifically:

- **Worship Attendance**: Your average attendance should be above fifty people and your goal should be to grow to above sixty. This is the threshold for survivability.

- **Baptisms**: There are two kinds of baptisms: biological and conversion. Biological baptisms are when children of members commit their lives to Jesus. If there are no biological baptisms it may mean there are few, if any children, at the church. Conversions are the result of your engagement with non-Christians, to help them overcome their unbelief and consider Jesus as a way of life. A church should always have at least one conversion baptism per year (one baptism for every fifty members, or 1:50), this is the minimum to maintain your current level of attendance. If you want to grow, your conversion rate must be at least 1:25. This will typically bring five or six new people to your church. Without conversion baptisms you should not expect to see any growth. Having conversion baptisms gets you on God's mission and indicates your church has the "stickiness" it needs to attract and keep new people.

- **Weekly Contribution**: The simplest interpretation is whether your weekly contribution is large enough to sustain your operations. That's the minimum. But you also need to dig deeper. I have met churches that have one or two exceedingly large givers who, by themselves, are able to keep the church operating. While the doors may be kept open, this mask's a level of unhealthiness in the church. That's why in question 8 above we look for at least 8 families who are giving generously. To truly be a healthy congregation the portion of the contribution devoted to missions and local outreach beyond the current membership should be 25-50% of your total budget.

- **Per Head Contribution**. The average donation by adults who attend U.S. Protestant churches is about $17 a week (NonprofitSource, 2018). That's $3,400 a month for a church of fifty attendees. To survive, this church cannot have any mortgage and will probably be on the life support of paying a guest speaker to preach for them each week. With other expenses, that's all this church can afford. A healthy church will typically be giving at twice the average rate, or somewhere around $35 per person. There is an interesting phenomenon, though. When a church becomes unhealthy and moves into the tanking zone of the church lifecycle the giving per person tends to become very high. I have seen per head giving as high as $150. The danger zone is somewhere around $60 per person, per week. Once giving reaches that stage it indicates the church is not reaching out and bringing in new people (who must be taught how to give). In church planting, the goals we suggested were for the church plant team to be giving $40 per person per week until they launch their regular Sunday services, then to see that drop to $20 per person per week over the next eighteen months as they bring more new people into their midst. At year five they should be back up above $30 per person per week.

Soft Numbers

Soft numbers are more personal and subjective than the hard numbers, but they are just as important. Here are four soft numbers that indicate what is happening inside you.

Instructions: Give a 1 (lowest) to 5 (highest) for each of these four items for where you are currently and where you think you should be six months from now if your church is pursuing a plan for better health and growth.

	Current	In 6 months
1. Anticipation of worship		
2. Energy for transition		
3. Optimism for your church		
4. Invitations made to church activities in the last 6 months		

- **Anticipation for Worship.** This item goes beyond the personal enjoyment of singing or being with longtime friends. This anticipation for worship is about expecting the presence and experience of God. It encompasses the genuine excitement of feeling God's presence, of hearing how God has been actively involved in the lives of brothers and sisters and seeing the difference God is making in your church, and through your church, your community.

- **Energy for Transition.** How is your energy level? How much gas do <u>you</u> have in <u>your</u> tank for the hard work of helping your church renew towards health and growth? We have found that this score is highest when people are younger, still in their family raising years. Once leaders have passed through this stage and into retirement, they no longer exhibit the energy and readiness to give the hours of work it takes to grow a church. It is particularly important for the leaders of the church to know they have the emotional, spiritual, and physical energy necessary to lead a church through a transition of renewal.

- **Optimism for your church.** It is possible for someone to have a high score here and low scores on the other three items. The key point here is that any move towards renewal must be based on reality. Naïve hope is not sufficient.

- **Invitations made to Church.** Churches grow best when its members are consistently and regularly inviting those around them to experience what they are experiencing. This should include invitations to special lessons and events at church, to small group meetings, to meals and coffee where the intentional topic is spiritual conversation. Making invitations opens the channels of communication while it opens our ears to hear better what our friends and relationships are thinking and feeling.

Decision: Redevelop or Repurpose?

By this point you should be developing an accurate picture of where your church is on the church lifecycle and a better sense of your capacity to engage an extended period of hard work to bring renewal and new life back to your church.

This last tool gives you the opportunity to summarize the ability and readiness of your church to plan for renewal and growth that can bring a new future of health to your church. Indicate a Yes or No beside each item

Membership	Building
1. ___ 50% of members involved in 5 or more church activities per month 2. ___ 3 or more families with elementary children	3. ___ Deferred maintenance is less than ½ annual contribution 4. ___ Fair Market Value of property is less than $10,000 per person
Leadership	Finances
5. ___ You have a full-time, high-capacity leader 6. ___ Decision-making capacity is high (not bound by minority veto)	7. ___ We can operate on our giving, without extra resources 8. ___ 80% of contribution comes from more than 8 giving units

- Membership

    1. Do at least 50% of your people attend church activities such as worship services and small groups at least five times per month?
    2. Do you have 3 or more families with elementary children in your church? This indicates your ability to draw and serve younger families who can form a new core within your church.

- Building

3. If you repaired all the deferred maintenance on your building, would it require less than half of your annual contribution?

4. FMV (Fair Market Value). Get an estimate of the fair market value of your property and divide that by your average Sunday worship attendance. If this calculation is greater than $10,000 per person, it shows your cost to continue meeting in your building is poor stewardship of kingdom resources.

- Leadership

    5. Do you have a full-time leader who has the abilities, time, and energy to lead a sustained charge towards a new future? This will typically be your preaching minister or a full-time elder.

    6. Is your church capable of making good decisions quickly? We find elderships often are stymied by one person who prevents the rest from making the decision they know is necessary. We call this the minority veto rule.

- Finances

    7. If you cannot operate without drawing from savings, rental, or other outside income your church is not able to pay for its continuing operation. Re-evaluate your stewardship.

    8. If 80% of your contribution does not come from 8 giving units or more, you are being kept on life support by a few key givers in your church. If they die or move it will leave you unable to continue.

To expect that you would be able to be one of the five percent of churches that can turnaround from tanking and experience a renewal or redevelop you must have at least six yeses.

Conclusion

This may have been a difficult chapter for you. Being willing to see reality is hard work. In the end, all I can do is give you the best opportunity to make the best decision possible for your church and God's kingdom.

If your church is in the tanking zone of its lifecycle and you really don't have the abilities to pursue an extended renewal process, don't rush out and proclaim that to your fellow leaders and members. Take some time to reflect and pray on what you have discovered here. Let God guide you in how to share your thoughts with your fellows. Investigate again together. Ultimately, the decision is yours to make. We want to be here to give you encouragement, good expertise, and help.

Reflection Questions

1. How would you describe the current state of your church in the church lifecycle?

2. Which of the four revitalization options do you think is most appropriate for your church? Why?

3. How do you think your church might best serve God's kingdom today?

4. What is your feeling about helping our fellowship of Churches of Christ for the future?

Scripture Study

Philippians 1:1-21

- When you reflect on the history of your church, what do you thank God for?

- How has your church been a partner in the gospel?

- When do you think your church had its maximum impact for the gospel? How did it do this?

CHAPTER 6 – LEADER RESPONSES

Here's a common church story. In the 1980s this was a large, dynamic church. They built a 500-seat auditorium that was filled every Sunday. Their two-story education center was a model for Sunday school education for their city and state. But over the years the neighborhood changed around them, their core leaders completed raising their families, the congregation aged, and the church drifted into the tanking zone of the church lifecycle.

Today this is a church of twenty-five to thirty members, all in their seventies or older, who meet in a corner of the auditorium on Sunday mornings to listen to sermons given by a rotating group of visiting preachers. On Wednesdays, the ten or so still able to drive at night meet around the former elders' conference table in the old church library.

The classrooms that once housed laughing, smiling children are silent, many still with the same signs on the doors and decorations on the walls that were put up thirty years ago. The church survives on the rent it receives from two houses on their property and renting out part of their education building to a small preschool.

One of their visiting preachers arranged for me to come and meet with their group one Wednesday and talk with them about options. These are wonderful people. They love each other and they love their church. My wife and I enjoyed getting to know them and listening to them speak about their church and its days gone by.

When we reached the point of talking about where they are today, I asked them why they are still trying to stay huddled together as this small remnant congregation in a building too big, too old, and too costly for them to care for. We asked about the several very good alternative churches in their area who would love to receive these few senior saints, how they could enjoy church life again with families and children, laughter, and joy.

The matriarch of the church looked around the table and answered, "Because we like each other. As long as we have rental income, we're fine just to stay together."

Why is it so hard for churches to close? There are many answers to this question. Let's explore what we hear leaders of small, declining churches at the end of their lifecycle say.

Not on my watch

This statement usually is spoken when there are still two or three men acting as elders over their small flock. In that situation there is often one man who believes it is his God-given duty to hold out at all costs. Often, his fellow elders are tired and worn out. They are looking for a way out that saves face and gives them some relief. But their beloved brother simply will not listen nor entertain any other thought. This church won't close "on my watch."

Theologically, Churches of Christ hold high the work of elders to guard, feed, and shepherd the flock, the church of Jesus (Acts 20:28). At our best, we accept this responsibility with a deep sense of accountability. Our elders feel, rightly so, that they will one day stand before the Lord Jesus to give account of how they led his church.

Practically, there is the sense of embarrassment that undergirds this "not on my watch" statement. Elders who are in their later years of retirement have often worked hard all their life. The idea of self-sufficiency is embedded deep in their psyche. The thought of the church closing is, well, it's embarrassing.

If you are feeling this way, let me give you permission to lay this burden down. We are so good at proclaiming ours is Jesus's church, yet sometimes we don't act that way. If Jesus demanded every church that ever started to live forever, then think of all those disappointments in Jerusalem and Rome and Corinth and every church ever mentioned in the New Testament. None of them have survived. Yet God's church still exists.

Jesus does want you to be faithful, but he doesn't expect you to perform miracles. His church will always continue, but it will do so in the forms and places that he chooses and blesses.

But where will people go to church?

This was the very first Church of Christ in the city. It was planted during World War II as the shipyards were filled with men building landing craft for the navy. The oldest member was a woman in her eighties whose parents were early members of the church. As the elders discussed the possibility of closing, this dear saintly woman asked, "But where will people go to church?"

It wouldn't be fair to try to guess her reasons for saying this. Was it theological, that our heritage is the only right and true church and others are not? Was it that she was comfortable in her church and felt others would be too? Or was it the sense of mission for her neighborhood? Whatever her reasons, the truth was people were not coming to this church and chances are they never would.

One of the historical motivations that drove our fellowship to plant new churches is the simple fact that we come from pioneer stock. Our fellowship has always had a strong westward expansion to it. Jerry Rushford wrote a marvelous exposition of our pioneering forbears in *Christians on the Oregon Trail* (College Press, 1997). We had men and women who looked around them and saw neighborhoods or communities where there really were no churches, so they moved to those new places and started churches in basements and barns, in grange halls and living rooms.

When we live out this pioneering spirit well, it drives us to start new churches in new places for new people. The spirit of the Macedonian call is strong within us. But sometimes that outward facing call gets turned around and it becomes an anchor rather than a sail. When we let God's call take us to the highways and byways of the world to preach the gospel and call the lost to God, I believe we live out our pioneering spirit as God intends it to be, as a blessing to the lost. But when that motivation gets turned around backwards it becomes a selfish and self-serving search for survival.

We need to be wise and careful to discern whether our desire to keep our church going is driven by God's mission or our own self-serving desires. The truth in answer to this question is that there are reasonable options in nearly every case if we are willing to open our eyes and see.

We got it right

I was raised in the church of the 1960s. It was a highly evangelistic time. The Jule Miller filmstrips were often heard dinging through homes, cottage meetings, and in classrooms around the building. Somewhere in all that goodness I picked up the idea that we were "the church." My job as an evangelist was to prove to anyone else that we were right, and they were wrong.

When I was in junior high, I ran into a group that was working the schools with Bible studies. I thought that was a good thing and started hanging around some of those conversations. One day I was introduced to their 21-year-old leader, Rick. Somehow, Rick got me into a personal Bible study with him about baptism. I was confident I had all the answers, so we were going to get it on. Rick ate my lunch that day—biblically speaking. He was a member of the Navigators, a high-powered, memorize scripture, lay it on the line group I didn't even know existed. I went home completely deflated, which gave my dad a great opportunity to walk me through the different perspectives Rick raised that day. My big takeaway from that experience was maybe we don't have all the answers.

As a Restoration Movement we have cut our teeth on the idea that our goal was to restore the New Testament church to its original pattern and correct practice. When this idea drives us back to scripture as our guide, it takes us good places. But it can also take us to the place of hubris, where we feel we are the only ones that have it right. We have the right name. We do things the right way. We are the church—the only church.

If we are the gold standard for Christianity, God help the world. Our fellowship is as fallible and susceptible to spiritual bends and twists as any other group. Are Churches of Christ good people? Most of the time. Are we trying to obediently follow God? Much of the time. Are we the only ones able to get it right? Experience and rationality would say no. Thinking that we are the only right church is not a valid reason for keeping a church open.

We don't need help

A while back I sent out a Heritage 21 email to a group of new leaders we had met. It was a simple email of introduction, sharing with them the Heritage 21 mission of helping churches plan their future and providing help to smaller churches. This elder replied, "We don't need help." I sent him another email as a note of encouragement, to which he said, "We don't want help."

These two statements, "We don't need help" and "We don't want help," communicate such different messages. Saying that we don't need help may indicate that we feel quite comfortable with the task—and we really are not at a point where help would make a difference. Or it can mean we don't know we need help. People can never do what they don't know to do. Sometimes we need a broader exposure to clue us in that we could use some help to do things better.

Saying we don't want help is very different. It reflects an attitude that is closed, that pushes others away. Refusing help may also reflect a sense of fearfulness. Sometimes we may feel that allowing people to help us means we are insufficient or not doing our job, so we reject the help for the sake of feeling good about ourselves.

I hope you don't feel that way. This world is far too complex and demanding for any of us to feel like we've got it all answered. We all need help, encouragement, and new ideas. That's what Heritage 21 seeks to provide. We want to help leaders get unstuck, to explore ways they can serve God and his kingdom well.

We have plenty of time

It takes churches a long time to die. The church lifecycle diagram with the traditional bell curve is somewhat misleading. The reality is the Tanking tail is often very, very long. Churches don't give up quickly. Sometimes that is good. With the right leadership and a lot of hard work sometimes a church does find a way to turn around and get a new lease on life. That's always a reason to rejoice. But most often, church leaders simply run out of ideas, so they just keep doing the same thing over and over.

What typically happens to a church in the Tanking phase is that people in the church grow tired. They slowly drift away. Capable men and women will often try to step in to bring energy and direction, but after a while they too grow tired and move to a more lively, active church. Then, the quality of leadership declines. We seldom see churches of fifteen, twenty-five or even fifty people that have capable leadership. In the worst-case scenario, a scoundrel comes in and takes control to make the church his, which sometimes means taking control of the church property as well. I know of a church that held on until only one family remained. They rented the building to a dance studio and used the rental income to fund their mother's retirement. We all believe nothing like that could ever happen at our church; but it does.

There often comes a time at the end of a church's life when the church no longer has the people or the capacity to make the good decisions they need to make. There is a timeliness to deciding that it is time to close a church.

Conclusion

In Jesus's parable of the talents in Matthew 25:14-30 Jesus presents a master who gives wealth to three servants, expecting each to steward that wealth for the master's benefit. We know the end of that story, where the one who did nothing, buried his wealth, and was punished.

A church's property is part of God's kingdom wealth. When a church has been blessed with land and building it is a gift of God for the church to use for God's good kingdom work. This wealth is not intended to exist in perpetuity. It is not to be hidden away to be preserved. Nor is the steward supposed to use it up until it is all gone, without worth to anyone else.

Every church needs to be faithful in its role as a steward of God's resources. As long as a church is using its wealth for God's work and His mission, it is good. But once a church reaches the point where all it is doing is surviving in order to keep a small remnant of people happy, it is no longer stewarding its resources well. There does come a point when a church's best stewardship decision is to sell its property and repurpose those resources to support other kingdom work.

Reflection Questions

1. Do any of these three leader responses resonate with you?

2. Choose one of these responses. How might you help someone get past this response in a helpful, healthy way?

Scripture Study

Matthew 25:14-30

- How might a church's real estate be like these talents?

- What might a church do to be a five or a two-talent church with their property?

- When might a church be in danger of being a one talent church?

PART 3: REDEVELOPMENT

In part 2 we looked at the lifecycle of churches and several tools you can use to assess your church's position on the lifecycle. The church lifecycle presents four revitalization options a church can take, each of them coming at a specific time in the lifecycle of the church. These four revitalization options are:

1. **Revision** can occur when a church is in its Booming or early Decelerating stages. Most churches need to revision every three to five years now.

2. **Renew** is best done in the middle or latter stages of Deceleration. In a renewal the church reforms itself at the core with a new sense of mission and vision.

3. **Redevelop** is an option when the church is in the Tanking stage. Redevelopment is essentially restarting the church as a new congregation. The existing church lets a new church grow in its place.

4. **Repurpose**, the church transitions itself out of its building and repurposes those resources for better kingdom advancement. Repurposing usually occurs when the church has unsuccessfully tried to renew and redevelop or has determined it does not have the resources to renew or redevelop.

In part 3 we're going to dive into a generic redevelopment process. Most churches I work with, even if they are deep into the tanking stage, seem to feel the need for one more try at revitalization. That wish is fine. It is good for a church to know it has done all it can to revitalize so if it repurposes it can do so with the sense that transitioning out of its real estate is the best stewardship decision it can make.

The redevelopment process has three primary parts to it: First is regaining the sense of mission that leads the church to evangelistically reach new people. When a church is tanking, gaining new people must happen. This will probably require the church to gain new evangelistic skills and habits.

Second is serving. Serving has two results. First, it helps address the negative perception people today share about Christianity and Christians as being bad. Second, it gives some very attractive invitation options where we can invite people to serve with us, putting us in talking distance with them.

Finally, there is discipling. Discipling has become a significant topic in the Christian world over the past ten years. The purpose of discipling is to teach people how to live faithfully across a lifetime.

There are a few reactions you will probably have as you read through these next three chapters. Your primary reaction is likely to be "This is hard work!" It is. To accomplish renewal or redevelopment requires churches to give up their maintenance mentality and learn to be missional in their thinking and actions. It is quite like starting a demanding physical fitness routine. At the beginning everything hurts. It takes time, effort and coaching to push past the beginning pains until the body gains the strength and mobility required. You can't expect to put on a new coat of paint here or add a new class there and be successful at renewal or redevelopment. It will need to be an all-hands-on deck effort with the determination to work at it for the next eighteen to twenty-four months.

When I worked with church planters planning to start a new church, we would tell them they would make three statements to their coach sometime along the way. I've found the same thing with churches trying to renew or redevelop. I suspect, if you choose one of these revitalization paths, that you will make these same statements.

1. **I don't know what to do**. None of us know everything we need to know. The response to the "I don't know what to do" statement is, "Who do you know who does?" Is there a church that is doing well that you can visit, talk with, use as an example? If you don't know what to do find someone who does! Stepping out on faith is a spiritual discipline church leaders need to practice.

2. **I don't know how to do it**. The answer to this statement is "Who is doing it well?" There is bound to be someone or some church who knows how to do well what you want to do. Learn from them.

Watch them. Let them train you. Become experienced in what you need to do. Seek answers from the Spirit through study and prayer.

3. **I don't want to do it**. At some time you might get to the point where you know what you ought to do and where to learn it, but you just don't want to do it. At this point you have two options. One option is you can look at what you are needing to accomplish and there may be another way to do it. If there is, go for it. The other option is to admit you simply don't want do it. If that is the case, then you need to make your plans to repurpose your church for better stewardship. At that point you can be confident you did everything you could to renew or redevelop. That should free you to sell your real estate to help some other kingdom projects and it lets your church transition into something more the right size or to close. This will be the subject of part 4.

CHAPTER 7 - EVANGELIZING

<u>Mis·sion</u> - *the vocation or calling of a religious organization, especially a Christian one, to go out into the world and spread its faith.*

In my experience as a missionary and in working with many churches, one of the tell-tale signs of a church that needs to renew is their loss of mission.

Often, the loss of mission begins by cutting the international missionaries out of the budget. The cry of, "We have to make sure we're stable at home so we can support missionaries" takes hold. Rationally, that statement is true. If the home church is weak or financially strapped it won't be able to keep supporting missionaries. But the real point is that a church that was once financially capable of mission support has lost that capability!

The problem is not the mission work, it's the state of the home church. It's the loss of mission at home that shows itself in redirecting missions abroad. The church forgets its mission is to seek and save the lost. The leaders and members become self and inward focused. People's thinking becomes protectionist. The budget turns its focus to "our needs" first.

This process of losing a sense of mission is called evangelistic entropy. Evangelistic entropy is described this way: *left to itself the value for evangelism will diminish to the point where it becomes normal <u>not</u> to reach out to people for Christ* (Rohrmayer, 2007). When a church experiences evangelistic entropy it loses both its motivation for and its capacity to share Jesus with those who are not yet believers. If you want your church to be healthy, sustainable, and able to grow you need to address your evangelistic entropy.

How can you tell if your church is suffering from evangelistic entropy? Here are three definitive signs:

1. **You haven't had at least one conversion baptism a year each of the last five years**. In a typical year the average church has at least one conversion baptism for every eighty attenders. This number has remained constant over the past fifty years. Conversion baptism

means the person being baptized isn't a family member (child or spouse); they are someone who previously wasn't connected to your church. This conversion rate of 1:80 is not good. It won't grow your church, but at least it gives you a starting point. Since many churches only have fifty to eighty attenders it means they should have at least one conversion baptism a year. If yours does not, you probably have evangelistic entropy.

2. **Your minister is not evangelistically active in the lives of lost people.** There was a time when we called our ministers "evangelists." I remember when ministers (and church leaders) took the role of evangelist seriously. They led the charge in having personal Bible studies, neighborhood door-knocking and conducting cottage meetings. Your minister should spend at least twenty percent of his time in evangelistic and outreach activities. That's one full day (and evening) every week. If your minister or pastor is not committed, or allowed, to regularly work evangelistically with people who are not part of your church, your church probably is experiencing evangelistic entropy.

3. **When asked about sharing their faith your people respond with, "I don't know how to teach someone about Jesus."** Really? How many sermons or Bible classes must a person sit through before they feel they can tell someone that Jesus is the best news ever! If your people don't feel like they can have significant spiritual conversations with their friends, neighbors, and coworkers your church will not grow. Do you remember the Jule Miller filmstrips (in our tribe), or Bill Bright's *Four Spiritual Laws* (among Baptists)? We used to train our people to use simple tools like these—and people were saved! If you want your church to grow to health you need to train your people to share Jesus with others.

Do You Believe It?

There is a cure for evangelistic entropy, and I believe it starts with a simple obedience check on three Bible verses. The obedience check asks, *Do I really believe what this verse says, and if I do, what I am determined to do about it?* Let's look at these verses.

John 3:16: *For this is how God loved the world: He gave his one and only Son, so that everyone who believes in him will not perish but have eternal life.*

Anyone who has any kind of church experience probably memorized John 3:16. It's just so simple and powerful, it draws us to its truths.

First, this passage roots us in the nature of God. God is love (1 John 4:16). God's love is good. It is enduring. It is active. God's love moves him to action. He doesn't just sit around in heaven hoping someone will notice his love. God proactively demonstrates His love for us over and over again.

Second, this passage takes us right to the climax of God's love story: Jesus. When someone loves another, that person will seek the best for the one he or she loves. That's exactly what God does here. He loves people so much he sent Jesus, his son, to save them.

Finally, John 3:16 tells us the result God wants because of his love: salvation. If God is making eternal life available, there must also be an opposite. If there is eternal life, there must also be eternal damnation. Do you believe this? Do you believe people who don't receive God's love through Jesus are going to hell? Do you want them to go to hell?

Your choice as a Jesus following church is to determine what you will do to make heaven an option to God's lost people. If God loves the world like this, and we are to be like God, then we've got to be lovers of people so much that we are willing to give and do so that they can be saved and not damned. That's strong stuff from a children's Bible class memory verse.

Luke 19:10: *For the Son of Man came to seek and save those who are lost.*

Your church has a mission given to you by King Jesus—and this verse gives it. Our mission as Jesus followers is to seek and save the lost. This is not a suggestion, a good idea, or something to go on your wish list. The reason your church exists is to fulfill God's mission to seek and save the lost.

There are three fundamental ways that churches fulfill this people-saving mission of King Jesus. First, as individual Christians we live lives of goodness that attract people to us and allows us to share our salvation story with them. Second, by supporting people who are gifted by God for evangelism, our ministers, and missionaries. Third, through church activities that introduce us to non-believers, followed by definite steps they can take to learn and decide what they want to do with King Jesus.

Acts 4:12: *There is salvation in no one else! God has given no other name under heaven by which we must be saved.*

One of the saddest turns among Jesus followers I've seen across my life is the prevalent rise of universalism, the belief that everyone will ultimately be save and restored to a right relationship with God. Universalism is not new, but the cultural pressures for tolerance and diversity make it so much more attractive to believe that God won't send anyone to hell and that there are many ways to salvation.

That's not what Peter preached, nor is it what he died for. Peter died because he believed that Jesus is the only person with the power to save. This is our confession that we make in baptism, that Jesus alone saves. If we believe this passage, then the only way people will be saved is for us to bring them to Jesus. That's our mission.

Here's how Paul takes these verses and weaves them into a plan of action:

^{14} But how can they call on him to save them unless they believe in him? And how can they believe in him if they have never heard about him? And how can they hear about him unless someone tells them? ^{15} And how will anyone go and tell them without being sent? That is why the Scriptures say, "How beautiful are the feet of messengers who bring good news!" (Romans 10:14-15).

These three verses—John 3:16, Luke 10:15 and Acts 4:12—are the powerhouse verses that describe what our churches should be about. Anything and everything else is secondary. Back to our obedience check. The obedience check asks, *Do I really believe what this verse says, and if I do, what I am determined to do about it?*

I assume you really do believe what these verses say. Now let's look at what you can do about it.

Everyone Is On A Spiritual Journey

Every person is on a spiritual journey through life. Some people know this, others don't. As people who are deeply attuned to spiritual things, we should be experts on people's spiritual journeys. I want to give you some simple, powerful insights into peoples' spiritual journeys so you can plan how your church can better accomplish King Jesus' mission.

In my church planting work, we often made the statement in training church planters that most people are three steps away from Jesus. We used the concept of a centered set to illustrate this to them. The centered set idea was developed by Paul Hiebert, a Christian anthropologist. Here is what a centered set looks like:

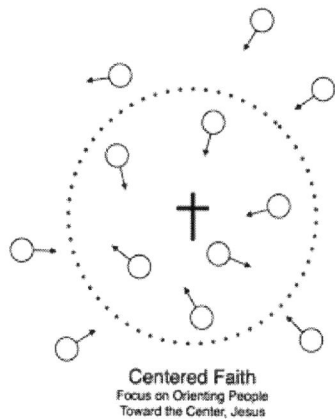

Centered Faith
Focus on Orienting People Toward the Center, Jesus

FIGURE 2. CENTERED SET.

A centered set is designed around a well-identified center. For us, that center is King Jesus. Jesus is both the object of the set and he is determinative criteria for evaluating one's state of being within the set. The centered set has three critical components to it: 1) direction, 2) distance and 3) commitment.

Direction is identified by arrows that either point towards Jesus or away from him. Every person is oriented in respect to Jesus. The person pointed away from Jesus is either unaware and unknowing, or they are not interested in Jesus. They need to see Jesus as an option to explore. When they make that decision, their arrow turns from pointing away from Jesus to pointing towards him. That's their first step, their first decision.

One of the missteps that we Christians make with people at this stage of their spiritual journey is we think if we can just get them to church or into a Bible study where they can learn about Jesus, they'll become Christians. But this part of the journey is not about knowing, it's about feeling. Right now, in America, there are many people who feel antagonistic towards Jesus. They don't like him. The last thing they want is to become a Christian. We need to pay attention to how people feel about Jesus so we can connect with them.

The evangelistic task for direction is gaining people's attention in a way that makes them curious about Jesus. We need to listen to people's objections with empathy. Sometimes they need space to vent before they'll ever be willing to listen. Our best opportunities are to be good examples, so they begin to wonder what is different about our life and theirs. Every person is in motion spiritually—at an angle toward or away from Jesus, or perhaps just gliding neutral at ninety percent. Our goal is to help them want to point their arrow in the direction of Jesus—and He will give the increase.

Distance indicates how far a person is from Jesus. If someone grew up in a Christian home, going to church, learning about the Bible they are likely to be close to Jesus. Someone who grew up without any exposure to Christianity will be a long way from Jesus. It is possible to be close to Jesus but to have one's arrow turn away from him. That typically does not happen all at once, but over time people who once followed Jesus drift further and further away until finally, their arrow turns.

Once someone has decided to turn towards Jesus our evangelistic task is to lead them closer to Jesus. This is where knowledge is important. Once people have emotionally decided Jesus is a valid option for their lives; they need to learn who Jesus was, what he taught, and how Jesus followers are expected to behave. Evangelistically this is the time for good Bible studies, often in groups, where the not-yet believer can ask questions without fear and to discuss implications for their lives.

Commitment is shown by the dotted line around Jesus. This line is the point of decision where the person decides to make Jesus King of their life. People can stand outside this line for a long time. Sometimes they are experimenting with living according to Jesus' expectations. Sometimes they are counting the cost, what they're going to have to change or give up to become a Christ follower. Sometimes they are waiting for others in their relationship network to make decisions.

Evangelistically, this is another emotional stage in the spiritual journey. We need to be tender, patient, and expectant of our friends who are in this process of becoming a Christian. I had a friend who stayed at this stage for four years. Every now and then I would ask her, "How are you doing? Are you ready yet?" She kept telling me no, not yet, until one day she called my wife to tell her she was ready. Our friend never told us what she was waiting on, but she knew we were patiently, expectantly waiting until she was ready to make her commitment in baptism.

The Journey to Belief

What is evangelism? I was raised with the idea that the purpose of evangelism was to convince another person to my way of belief. That immediately put me into the stance of an aggressor and the other person was the defender. My task was to intellectually beat the other person into submission until they would admit their view was wrong and mine was right. Honestly, that didn't feel good for either side, and it may be a significant reason why so many Christians simply refuse to consider evangelism in their lives.

There is another, a better and more biblical, framework in which to understand evangelism. That is the role of spiritual guide. This is the role Philip (who later was called "the evangelist") enacted with Nathanael in John 1:43-51; Philip guided Nathanael to Jesus. If every person is on some kind of spiritual journey, as we explored above, and if we Christians are more practiced at that spiritual journey than most people, then we should be able to act as guides to others less practiced in spiritual ways.

Being a spiritual guide to others is a much more palatable and friendly approach to evangelism than the aggressor/defender roles that were once held up as the model for me. In Celtic Christianity, this idea of being a spiritual guide was described by their word *anamchara,* which means "soul friend" (Tippens, *Pilgrim Heart*, 2006). As Christians we are to be *soul friends* to those we are bringing to Jesus.

What does a spiritual guide, a soul friend do? First, a soul friend is curious about what is happening in the life of the other. A soul friend asks questions and helps make connections. Second, a soul friend listens attentively and helps clarify the questions the other is asking. Finally, a soul friend sees the work of God in the life of the other and brings that work into the light so the other can begin to see how deeply God is engaged with them.

Personally, I find the role of evangelist as a spiritual guide, or soul friend, much more satisfying and culturally appropriate than the idea of an evangelist as a debater.

How do we do the work of an evangelist as a spiritual guide or soul friend? Let me share with you three spiritual conversation tools I have used hundreds if not thousands of times through the years that are simple and easily doable. I have taught these tools to many people. Those who have used them have been amazed at how God has opened opportunities for them to share Jesus with others. You will find these and other tools in my self-guided study *Leading Others: Sharing Faith* (2015).

3 Question Conversation

For many Christians, the idea of having a spiritual conversation with someone about Jesus is scary. We don't have much (if any) experience with it and our church probably doesn't ever talk about it. But if we are going to reach new people with the good news of Jesus, we need to learn how to start healthy spiritual conversations with them. That's what the 3 Question Conversation does, it opens spiritual conversations.

Here's how the 3 Question Conversation works:

Question #1 – The Polite Question. When you meet someone, you probably ask a polite question, something like: "How are you doing?" What's Up?" or "What's going on?" All these are safe, socially acceptable questions. Usually, we're not really looking for an answer; we're just recognizing the other person is there. For most of us this is where we stop. We've carried out our polite, social responsibility and we don't feel any further obligation. But what if we take our role as a spiritual guide seriously? What if we believe God really seeks out people and works in their lives calling them to him and we are truly curious about what God may be doing in this other person's life? What would we do? We don't stop with question one; we move on to the second and third questions.

Question #2 – The Interest Question. This question should be something that is relevant to the situation. If you're standing in line at the grocery store it could be, "Do you shop here often, how do you find this store?" If it's at a sporting event with children an obvious question is, "Which child are you here with, how are they doing?" If it's related to school, it could be, "How is your child's schooling going?"

The Interest Question has two important effects. First, it demonstrates that you have an interest in the other person. Since most people stop at the Polite Question, the Interest Question catches people's attention. It immediately signals that this conversation is going to be different. Second, it serves as a transition question. It moves the conversation from the public sphere to the private sphere. When you ask this second question you are letting the other person know that you are interested in them (you are, right?) and you are offering a point of connection.

Question #3 – The Caring Question. The Caring Question is the gold mine. This question signals the other person that not only are you interested in them, but you really care about them. Before you ask the Caring Question, share something about yourself. If you've asked who their child is on the ball field, point out your own child. Add an extra piece of information such as your child's name, school, or how long your child has been on the team. If you've asked about their child at school, share something about your child at school. This extra information helps establish you as a safe person, which is important in our on-guard, stranger danger society. After you've shared something personal, ask your third question.

Where the Polite and Interest Questions stuck to the facts, make your Caring Question about feelings. "Are you feeling good about your child's experience?" "Do you feel like this is a good environment?" "Does this situation feel like a positive one for you?"

When you ask the Caring Question, be prepared to hear something amazing. People may tell you some of the most intimate and life-challenging pieces of information. I've had people tell me about divorces, run-away children, terminal illnesses, and so much more. Why would people do this? Why would strangers almost rush to share these intimate details about their lives with you? I see two reasons. First, few people today actually listen to others. People are surprised by and hungry for a listening ear. Second, people no longer have safe places to talk about the deep issues of life. We aren't supposed to get personal at work. Homes are often places of emotional trauma. Friendships are built around fun. Pushing to a deeper level with friends can endanger the relationship or open opportunities for betrayal. If people sense you are offering them a safe space for conversation, many times they will jump at it.

Don't stop with this third question. As amazing as your conversation may be, there's one more thing to do. Here it is. Invite the other person to sit down with you to continue the conversation. Do this with this simple invitation: "I've really enjoyed visiting with you. I'd love to hear more of your personal story. Could we get coffee together so we could talk more?

This is a big step for that other person. Don't be surprised if they pause to think through this. They'll be thinking about how they feel about you and your current conversation. They'll have to think about their schedule, their work, their family, and their friends. They'll have to decide whether they want to try out a new relationship. They're processing a lot. Don't feel like you must push. You've made the offer. If you feel they are very hesitant say something like, "I know you'll have to really look at your schedule. Here, let me give you my cell number. Maybe we can touch base later this week. Would you mind sharing your cell number with me?" Thank them well at that point and let that conversation soak.

5 Bucket Spiritual Diagnosis

When Jesus met the Samaritan woman at the well (John 4) a conversation began around how to get a drink of water from the well, moved into a discussion on religion, and ended with Jesus delving into her personal lifestyle choices. Talk about a confrontational, spiritual conversation. Yet this conversation changed this woman's life. In fact, she became an evangelist who shared Jesus with her entire village! What Jesus did with her was a spiritual diagnosis. He listened to her (4:7-15), dug into her beliefs and life practices (4:16-26), and gave her the opportunity to respond (4:27-30, 39-42).

If we're going to guide people on their spiritual journey, we need to understand their starting point. If they are not yet believers, why not? This is what a spiritual diagnosis is; it is discovering why the other person is not yet a believer. There are five primary reasons why North Americans don't believe. I call these reasons "buckets." Let's look at these five buckets of unbelief.

Bucket #1 – Intellectual. Many people who are unbelievers, see religion in general and Christianity specifically, as not intellectually reasonable. They've been taught that science has the answers and is the only plausible explanation. Religion for them is a folk tale that is simply not believable.

Those who don't believe because of intellect may also see the classic question "how could a good God allow suffering" as unanswerable for Christians. It seems obvious to them that the presence of suffering means that God is either not caring enough or not powerful enough to eliminate suffering (particularly the suffering of babies and innocents). Either way, why should they buy into that kind of God?

Finally, unbelievers who fall into the intellectual bucket of unbelief look at the Christian church across history and see it responsible for so much injustice in history that it has no more credibility.

Bucket #2 – Lifestyle. People do make lifestyle choices that prohibit belief. Sometimes they choose these lifestyles to demonstrate they don't believe. The lifestyle choices are often culturally sensitive topics that involve choices of sexual behavior, dress, and even professions. A person who has chosen a lifestyle that stands against Christian belief and lifestyle has invested a significant portion of their self-identity into that lifestyle. As spiritual guides we need to listen well to them to understand why they made that choice and how it wraps around their sense of self.

Bucket #3 – Oppression. Oppression includes events or circumstances such as family of origin issues, dependencies, addictions, and even personality disorders and personal traumas. There is a distinct difference between lifestyle and oppression. Where lifestyle issues are choices people make, oppressions are outside their control. People who grew up in an abusive home had no choice in how they were treated, but they bear deep scars that may harden them against belief in God. The result of oppression is often a hardness of spirit that prevents God's seed from taking root.

Bucket #4 – Bad Experiences. There are two kinds of bad experiences involved here. The first are bad life experiences, events such as accidents, illnesses, and the loss of loved ones in death. These kinds of experiences are often expressed by a statement like, "I cannot believe in a God who would allow . . ." The second kind of bad experiences are bad encounters with Christians. Stories abound of Christians who acted so unkindly or uncaring that those who experienced them say, "I never want to be like that."

Bucket #5 – No Knowledge. Amazingly, there is an ever-growing number of North Americans who simply have no real knowledge or experience of Christianity. All they know is what they hear from their friends and an increasingly anti-Christian media via television, entertainment, and social media.

In conducting a spiritual diagnosis, you are a listener who is asking good questions. You want to create a safe space that allows people to express their feelings and ideas without fear of reprisal, ridicule, or opposition. Your goal as spiritual guide is not to argue them out of their bucket. Your purpose is to give them the opportunity to explore their personal bucket of unbelief. Eventually, after a lot of emotion and words, if you are patient, they will ask you, "What do you think?" That's when you can begin to share your perspective as a follower of Jesus.

The "My Spiritual Journey" Napkin

If you use these spiritual conversation tools, here's what's happened to this point. First, you've met a total stranger and initiated a budding relationship with them. You've offered them the opportunity to pursue a new relationship with you. If you've been able to get together for that coffee invitation you've heard a lot more of their story and you've done an initial spiritual diagnosis. So, what's next?

Typically, if you get one or two coffee times together, the other person will eventually ask, "What about you?" Now that they've shared a lot about themselves and used a lot of words, their curiosity about you will build. At that point you can share with them who you are, that you're a believer in Jesus, and that talking about spiritual things is important to you.

My friend Gary Rohrmayer wrote a little pamphlet called *Your Spiritual Journey Guide.* It is an excellent spiritual assessment tool to help seekers and believers alike determine where they are spiritually and to show them how to take the next steps on their spiritual journey.

The *Your Spiritual Journey Guide* is intended for use in sit down conversations. Sitting down is a talking posture. Your role is to ask a few key questions and listen, listen, listen. Remember *Your Spiritual Journey Guide* is a spiritual diagnostic and planning tool. You're not doing a Bible study yet.

Once you get seated, thank the person for his or her willingness to share their spiritual journey with you. This sets up the topic and shows respect. Then take a napkin and draw this diagram on it.

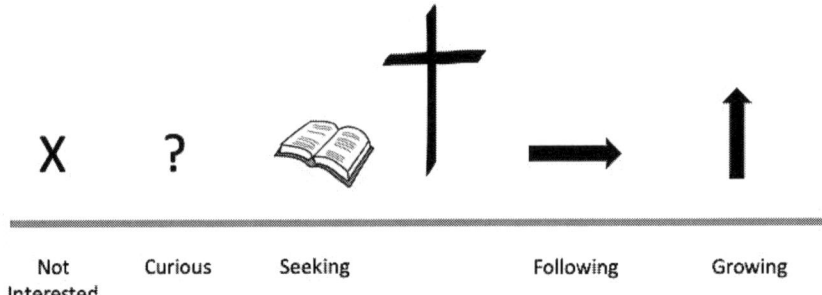

FIGURE 3. YOUR SPIRITUAL JOURNEY.

As you draw this diagram on the napkin, explain each of the stages something like this:

1. **Not Interested.** I know this is not you because we're here together talking about your spiritual journey.

2. **Curious.** When they are curious, people have a lot of questions about Jesus, Christianity, and church.

3. **Seeking.** People who are seeking often know quite a bit about Jesus, but there are questions or ideas that bother them or don't make sense.

4. **Following.** This is where people make a public commitment to follow Jesus and we want to encourage them to connect to a church.

5. **Growing.** Here is where people are regularly doing what you and I are doing now. They are encouraging each other in life, reading and sharing the Bible together, and praying for each other.

Once you've drawn the spiritual journey line ask the other person these questions:

1. Where do you see yourself now on this spiritual journey? Give them your pen and ask them to mark an X where they see themselves. This gives you both a visual marker to help make the discussion more real. When they make their mark, they are doing their own spiritual diagnosis about their relationship to Jesus.

2. Where would you like to be on your spiritual journey six months from now? When you ask this question, you are inviting the other person to deliberately think about and plan their personal spiritual journey. Invite the person to make a second X at the point he or she would like to be in six months.

3. What is standing between you and that point? This question helps the person identify barriers against faith in her life. This is where she will reveal her reasons for not believing (her buckets of unbelief). These answers will confirm or adjust the spiritual diagnosis you have done in your head. By recognizing these faith barriers, you are building the expectation that her current situation can change. You are also helping her develop her own personalized plan for spiritual discovery.

4. How could I help you on your spiritual journey? This is your final question. You are continuing to extend your hospitality as a spiritual guide. You also provide the opportunity for her to think about next steps. At this point she may need you to introduce her to more resources. Typical resources could be a readable modern translation of the Bible (often non-Christians have a King James Version as the only Bible available to them), an invitation to a social gathering with other Christians, or to be part of a discipleship group.

This entire conversation can typically occur in about forty-five minutes. Keep it moving forward. Be aware of the time so you do not overextend her interest or time availability. Finally, always leave the conversation with the open invitation for the next step.

When time is up, sincerely thank the person for sharing her spiritual journey with you, her barriers to faith, and her ideas on next steps. If she seems unwilling to commit to a next step at that time, ask her permission to send her information on events and opportunities that your church is doing.

How Will Evangelism Impact Your Church?

My assumption is that your church is on the small size (below seventy-five), slowly declining, and your members may be mostly older. You've done your assessment and you are wanting to see your church be healthier and capable of a longer life. How will developing your evangelistic activity help you achieve these goals?

You will see God at work
If you asked your people why they come to church, how would they answer you? Many will say to obey God—and that's a good answer. Others will say because of the encouraging fellowship. That's also a good answer. Other answers people often give as to why they go to church are to create a moral foundation for their family, because of the worship, to be closer to God, and to become a better person.

When your church is evangelistically active you will see God at work. God's work is an amazing reason for people to come to your church. When you are engaged in guiding people to believe in Jesus you will get to see how God has worked in their lives. One of our friends, who became a Christian later in life, began her journey saying she had never seen God in her life and didn't believe God existed. A year later she sat with our small group in tears relating to us multiple amazing moments in her life when now, through the lens of belief, she saw God at work in her life. As an evangelistically active church you will get to hear—and experience—those stories over and over again.

Move from Maintenance to Missional
People who work broadly with churches in America consistently tell us that eighty percent of churches exist in a maintenance mode. Maintenance churches are focused on doing the same things they have always done with the goal of keeping their people happy. As long as the doors of the church are open and their friends are coming, life is good.

We saw earlier that God is not a God of maintenance. He is a God of mission. It seems reasonable to assume that if God is a missional God, He is not that excited about maintenance churches. In fact, the church at Laodicea (Revelation 3:14-22) was feeling pretty comfortable as a maintenance church. God told them, *[15] I know all the things you do, that you are neither hot nor cold. I wish that you were one or the other! [16] But since you are like lukewarm water, neither hot nor cold, I will spit you out of my mouth! [17] You say, 'I am rich. I have everything I want. I don't need a thing!' And you don't realize that you are wretched and miserable and poor and blind and naked.* When your church is evangelistically active you are obeying the missional mandate of God to *Go into all the world* (Matthew 28:18-20).

New People will be Added
The purpose of evangelism is to help people move from unbelief to belief. Luke gets very succinct about these results in Acts 2:41: *Those who believed what Peter said were baptized and added to the church that day.*

There are three ways that churches grow. First, a church can depend on transfer growth, Christians who move into the neighborhood and choose that church as their home church. While transfer growth is helpful, it does not represent actual kingdom growth. Then there is biological growth, baptizing children of Christian families. But biological growth is very slow, and if the church members are beyond childbearing years, they have no biological growth potential. Finally, there is conversion, or evangelistic, growth. Conversion growth is always available; it is the real transference of people from the kingdom of darkness to God's kingdom of light (Colossians 3:16). There is no better way for your church grow than to have new believers added to your church body.

Newness will Enter Your Church
I often ask ministers who are struggling with a maintenance mindset in their church how families get new blood. They'll usually pause a few seconds, then say, "Marriage!" That's right. The only way to bring new DNA into the family system is through marriage (or, of course, adoption). The same is true with churches. Transfer and biological growth don't bring new blood, new DNA, into the church. Newness enters a church with new people!

When new believers enter your church, they will ask new questions. They'll ask why you do things the way you do. They'll wonder about other ways of "doing church." Their questions are sometimes naïve, but always worthy of thought. And, when a new person becomes a Christian, they typically will lead you to two or three other people who might also become new Christians. New growth produces more new growth!

How Do I Help My Church Become Evangelistically Active?

If you are serious about leading your church to new health and revitalizing it, you must lead your church to become evangelistically active. There is no other God-given, God-approved way to do this. Here are three starting point activities for you to do.

First, find ways to evangelistically pray for your church, your neighbors, and your community. Ask God to bring you people who are ready to hear! Organize your members to do prayer walks in your church neighborhood. So often members of older, dying churches only see their neighborhood through their car window. A car is a safe barrier. When you prayer walk your neighborhood, you will see it differently. You'll probably actually begin to see the people God wants you to see, and you may get to meet them.

Second, release your minister to spend twenty percent of his time for outreach and evangelism, and expect it. When your minister is meeting new people and having spiritual conversations with them you will hear it in his preaching and teaching. Those new stories of God at work will leak out from him.

Third, tell the stories of spiritual conversations with people and publicly celebrate how you see God at work. The phrase, "celebrate what you want," is very true for a church. I've seen churches that only do baptisms after the service or as a private ceremony. I do understand that sometimes people are very shy and want to be baptized privately. But if your people never see anyone being baptized, if you don't make a big deal out of new life in baptism, the message you give your people is baptisms are no big deal.

Reflection Questions

1. How would you describe the evangelistic temperature of your church?

2. How many people has your church baptized in the last 5 years? How many of these were biological and how many were conversion baptisms?

3. Are you currently encouraging and training your members to engage others in spiritual conversations? If not, how can you use ideas here to train them?

Scripture Study
Romans 10:14-17

- What do you think Paul means by "preaching" in v. 14? What kinds of ways can we engage in preaching that is beyond someone standing in the pulpit?

- Who are the people in your church whom you would describe as having "beautiful feet?" Why do you think of them?

- How have you experienced or seen the power of the word of Christ working in people's lives?

CHAPTER 8 - SERVING

Serving the world is an absolute must for churches today. As we discussed in chapter 2, America has experienced a deep cultural change that is aggressively anti-Christian. This means that we believers begin spiritual conversations with non-believers from a negative starting point. If we are going to expect them to hear us, we must first earn the right to be heard, then we must demonstrate that our message has validity. This is one reason why churches must be actively engaged in serving activities in our neighborhoods, cities, and the world. Service gives us credibility as people who might possibly not be bad, and it provides an attractional force for potential new believers.

Another reason is that our younger generations, particularly those under thirty-five years old, are deeply oriented towards humanitarian service. For them, to do good is often a higher value than doing church. For them, a church that does not actively address the needs of the world loses its credibility as an instrument of God and its worthiness for membership. These are hard words to accept. But if churches planted in the 20th century are going to claim relevance among our 21st century generations, these are the terms we will need to live by.

Service and Servant Evangelism

The concept of godly service is a biblical centerpiece. The people of Israel were commanded to care for strangers among them because they were once strangers (Exodus 22:21). Jesus, in the Golden Rule, said, *"Do to others whatever you would like them to do to you"* (Matthew 7:12). The prophet Isaiah spoke of the suffering servant in chapter 53. Jesus said, *"For I was hungry, and you fed me. I was thirsty, and you gave me a drink. I was a stranger, and you invited me into your home."* These verses are all expressions of a witness to the love and compassion of God through the kindness his people show to others.

The term "servant evangelism" was coined in 1985 by Steve Sjogren, founding pastor of Vineyard Community Church in Cincinnati, Ohio. Vineyard Community grew from thirty-seven to over six thousand people over the course of a decade. In his book *Conspiracy of Kindness* (2014) Sjogren defined servant evangelism as *demonstrating the kindness of God by offering to do some acts of humble service with no strings attached.* His premise is that if we are willing to participate in acts of love and kindness to those outside our circle, through those humble acts of service, God's love will plant a seed that has the chance to blossom into faith.

Serving can be done in so many ways—by passing out quarters at laundromats, offering free car washes, conducting light bulb and soda giveaways, even cleaning toilets. In fact, Sjogren developed a list of *Ninety-Four Servant Evangelism Ideas for Your Church.*

Kind actions, however, are not sufficient. We do good things because God is good, and we are his people. However, if we stop at doing good, we miss our opportunity to speak about God's goodness. This speaking about God's goodness is what turns service into service evangelism.

Putting evangelism in the context of service, however, puts us in a bit of an emotional bind. It's admirable to do good, and many people will want to do good with us. But when we bring Jesus into the picture, they can feel like they've encountered a bait and switch tactic, as if we're saying, "I'll do something good if you'll let me tell you about Jesus." That's not the feel we want to create. The kind of service we want to do is the kind that will raise questions about why we are doing it.

Recently I was talking with the leader of a new campus ministry in a west coast university. After eighteen months of Covid isolation, with no students on campus, it seemed like almost everyone was new. This campus ministry served students in a variety of ways, including a very special international meal and game night. Over fifty students showed up, most of whom were not Christians. As the meal was served these students were curious as to who was paying for it. They were stunned to know that there were Christians from different states who were so caring that they would pay for meals for students whom they would never meet because they were Jesus's people. This is a picture of the kind service evangelism your church needs to practice. It is not a bait and switch, but it does allow us to begin spiritual conversations with the people we serve and those who serve with us.

How, then, should we approach servant evangelism? Let's look at three levels of compassionate activity that eventually arrive at servant evangelism.

Acts of Kindness

First, let's talk about kindness. You may have heard the phrase "random acts of kindness," in which we're encouraged to do something kind for others, like purchasing a latte for the customer behind us at Starbucks. Christians are supposed to be living representatives of God, Jesus, and the Holy Spirit. One characteristic of the Godhead is kindness. In Psalm 136 David repeats the phrase "*His loving kindness endures forever*" over and over again. We should practice kindness because it's who we are. It's the nature of godliness to do good. Doing good is a by-product of our new life in Jesus (Galatians 6:9-10). I appreciate what Steve Sjogren says, "I have become kind of hooked on showing people generosity, kindness, and respect whenever I get the chance."

Acts of Service

The next level up is service. Service occurs when we become deliberate about our acts of kindness, often at the corporate level of the church body. Examples of service activities that churches do are operating a food bank, engaging with homeless camps as a sponsor, or adopting a low-income population school. At the level of service, we are compassionate, caring people like our father in heaven. But additionally, we believe when the kingdom of God breaks into the world, the world should become a better place. When John the Baptist was feeling doubts about Jesus as Messiah, Jesus sent this reply of proof back to John, *the blind see, the lame walk, those with leprosy are cured, the deaf hear, the dead are raised to life, and the Good News is being preached to the poor* (Matthew 11:2-6). Establishing hospitals and clinics in Haiti, digging freshwater wells in Africa, and adopting child activities in South America all arise out of this kingdom mind set of making the world a better place.

Servant Evangelism

The final level of service is servant evangelism. Kindness and service become servant evangelism only when we deliberately attach a message about faith to our actions. I know from personal experience in Africa that if we don't tell people why we are doing good works they will make up their own reasons, and those reasons will probably bear little resemblance to ours. How do we attach words of Jesus to our acts of kindness and service so they create opportunities to share Jesus? Begin with confessions of faith.

Confessions of faith don't have to be huge. Confessions of faith can be as simple including the name and website of your church on the labels of the water bottles you are handing out at a local running event, setting up an A-frame sign that says, "Provided by Lighthouse Church" when you are cleaning up a public park, or leaving a contact card printed with your church's web address and "Call us when we can serve you next" when you help a neighbor with their house.

What is the purpose of servant evangelism? First, servant evangelism works against the common belief of American society that churches don't contribute to a better life. The mayor of New Brunswick, New Jersey, said of the Brunswick Church of Christ, "When we think of a church that helps our community, we think of you." The work a church does in a town can soften the attitudes of unbelievers they meet.

Second, practicing servant evangelism as a church enables the congregation to engage their community on the community's terms. It gets us outside our building where we can meet people, deliberately and with purpose. The Renovo church in Puyallup, WA ran a face-painting booth with free helium balloons every weekend at their local Farmers' Market. While one person painted the child's face, another offered the parents an opportunity to have a spiritual conversation and to complete a contact card to receive information from Renovo, if they wished. Renovo grew numerically more from this one, repeated activity than anything else they did.

Three Steps to Servant Evangelism Impact

How can your church begin the service component of your church life? Use what I call the three-step approach. My experience is most not-yet-believers are three steps away from you and your church building. Rather than expecting them to make a huge jump between where they are to where we are, the three-step approach gives them smaller steps they can take more easily.

Step 1: Do THEIR things in THEIR places
When you think of growing your church, your first thought may be, "how can we get people to come to us?" Instead, ask, "Where do the people gather whom we want to reach?" When you do that, you are helping them do their activities (their things) under their organizational banner (their places). Start by taking an inventory of what is happening in your neighborhood or community. Find out what events are taking place in area schools. What are your local service agencies, chamber of commerce, and schools doing? Go to their events and join in. When you do this, you go as a guest in their space. You should be circumspect about what you say about your faith. In their space, play by their rules. This shows respect and builds trust.

Step 2: Do THEIR things in OUR places
At this step you will do some of the same things people in your community are already doing (their things), but now you take on the organizational role to extend that service or activity into new areas, communities, or to new people. Becoming the organizing force is what makes it "our places." By "our places" I'm not talking about geographic place (our church building) but ownership. Some activities I've seen churches do are providing a weekly meal in a local park to homeless teens, cleaning and providing meals in a women's shelter, and organizing a tutoring program at the nearby elementary school. All these activities were already being done in some way. But when you become the organizer, you take a load off the people working in those activities. You relieve them to do other things they need to do that you can't do. That's how you help!

When you become the organizer don't expect the people you are serving to be the ones you impact the most. Typically, the people you will have the most opportunity to get to know and influence are those who have been working those activities and the people you invite to serve with you. This is critical. These kinds of activities are golden opportunities to invite people who would never accept an invitation to come to your church building. But to come along to do something good for people—they're all into that! When they join with you to serve, they should pick up easily that you are Christians and that your church is organizing this activity. When they know that fact and still join you, they have voluntarily stepped over the line into your space. Once they have entered your space you have much more opportunity to speak to them about why you are doing this service ... because of Jesus. This is your confession of faith.

Step 3: Do OUR things in OUR places.
What I mean by "do OUR things in OUR places" is that both the idea and the ownership are ours. These are activities that characterize us, and we organize them. These are the spaces in which we overtly display and practice our Christian faith. These are our small groups or house churches, our church picnics and fellowship activities, our worship services, and our prayer times. We do these things because we are Christians, and these activities are part of our Christian lifestyle.

When we invite not-yet-believers to do OUR things in OUR places they know they are in our space. When people make this third step, we should be confident in asking them about their spiritual lives and engaging them in spiritual conversations. After all, when you go to a doctor's office you don't expect to talk about the weather and sports then go home. You've gone there because you have a physical question or issue. When people join you in your Christian activities, they know you're going to talk about spiritual questions and issues. By joining you in doing your things in your places they are giving you explicit permission to share faith with them.

I hope you understand how important and how easy it is for your church to be a serving church in your community. But, if your church does not have a track record of serving, if the extent and focus of your church's activities is to meet Sunday mornings, Sunday evenings and Wednesday evenings, don't expect your church members or even your fellow church leaders to accept the idea of service easily. They won't. They've been trained to believe that their job is to hold services and do things the right way. You will have to convince them that the health and future of your church will be dependent on making service an essential spoke in your church's life wheel.

Reflection Questions

1. Why is serving for the good of humanity critically important for churches today?

2. How would you explain the difference between service and servant evangelism?

3. What areas of service is your church already engaged in? What percentage of your people are involved in at least four service activities per year?

4. Look at the *3 Steps to Servant Evangelism*. Describe something your church could do for each step.

    a. Their things in their places

    b. Their thing in our places

    c. Our things in our places

Scripture Study

Acts 3:1-4:4

- What step in the *3 Steps to Servant Evangelism* do you see this story beginning with?

- When do you think it turned into servant evangelism, or did it?

- What was the message Peter told the crowd?

- What kinds of reactions did Peter and John provoke from those who heard and experienced this event?

CHAPTER 9 - DISCIPLING

The word disciple (Greek: *mathetes*) is used in some form 269 times in the New Testament. In its most general use, disciple describes the relationship between a teacher, or master, and a student (Matthew 10:24-25a). In reference to Jesus, a disciple described anyone who followed Jesus as he taught and healed and fed (John 6:66). And most specifically, the 12 apostles of Jesus were called disciples (Matthew 10:1).

What I find quite interesting is that the New Testament wraps the idea of disciple in the context of Jesus. These 269 disciple words are only used in the gospels and in Acts. The word for disciple isn't used by Paul, or Peter, or James or in the three letters from John or his book of Revelation. Evidently, the idea of Jesus walking by the Sea of Galilee and calling Peter, Andrew, James, and John to *Follow me, and I will make you fishers of men* (Matthew 4:18-22), was so deeply imprinted as the core of discipleship that the biblical writers didn't use that word apart from the presence of Jesus. That's amazing!

The Mission of Discipling

When I was growing up in the 1960s and 1970s, I seldom heard the term "discipling" in my church. Probably what I heard that carried the idea was "being a good Christian." When I did hear a lot about discipleship and disciple-making was with the rise of International Churches of Christ under the leadership of Kip McKean as a discipling movement. It didn't take long for the divisive undertones and cult-like expressions of this discipling movement to drive a wedge into our fellowship that created two distinct entities of Churches of Christ. Sadly, out of that division the idea of discipleship and discipling garnered a bad reputation within our tribe, a negative vibe that still resonates among us.

Yet disciple, discipleship and discipling are biblical concepts. For a people who take some pride in "calling Bible things by Bible names," it seems inappropriate for us to dismiss these words because of a bad experience.

Leading for Discipleship

[11] Now these are the gifts Christ gave to the church: the apostles, the prophets, the evangelists, and the pastors and teachers. [12] Their responsibility is to equip God's people to do his work and build up the church, the body of Christ. [13] This will continue until we all come to such unity in our faith and knowledge of God's Son that we will be mature in the Lord, measuring up to the full and complete standard of Christ (Ephesians 4:11-13).

How do we make disciples? Mike Breen rightly proposes that this question is at the core of every other question we hear about the church in our world (*Building A Discipling Culture*, 2017). Equipping and maturing Christ's disciples is one of our three primary tasks as church leaders. Disciple making is a significant part of what our gatherings are to accomplish. Yes, we are to worship. Yes, we are to fellowship. But we are also to equip and mature disciples. As we saw above, at its core, Christian discipleship means to follow and learn from Jesus. Discipling is *helping people to follow and obey Jesus*.

How do we know if we're being successful at equipping and maturing disciples? For many leaders what they have been taught, by osmosis, example, or experience, is that good disciples come to church when the doors are open, they give to the church, and they don't cause the elders problems. These are certainly measurable and positive attributes, but I've known some bad church people who lived up to these measures. I have a friend whose husband was a terrible man, abusive and just plain mean. He attended church, gave to the church, and didn't cause the elders problem, but it would be very hard to call him a mature disciple of Jesus.

There are all sorts of activities and behaviors that can be associated with mature disciples but trying to keep track of a laundry list is overwhelming. Here are three characteristics that summarize the heart of mature disciples.

First, a mature disciple is **committed to Jesus**. We saw in John 6:66 that it was the immature, the under-committed disciples who quit following Jesus when the heat turned up. The committed disciple knows that commitment to Jesus as Lord and King isn't an on today, off tomorrow proposition. It's all or nothing and 24/7. Mature disciples make life decisions thinking first about their commitment to Jesus, not about their promotion or upcoming vacation. Mature disciples live by Jesus' choices.

Second, a mature disciple is **obedient to Jesus**. Jesus told his first disciples, *Therefore, go and make disciples of all the nations, baptizing them in the name of the Father and the Son and the Holy Spirit. Teach these new disciples <u>to obey all the commands I have given you</u>* (Matthew 28:19). Obedient disciples live like Jesus, and they talk about Jesus. By living like Jesus, obedient disciples create opportunities to share their experiences of Jesus, express what they are learning from him. I often shared with our church planters that if they did not confess their faith to a new person the first or second time they met them, it would probably only be by chance that that person would ever learn they were a Jesus follower. Obedient disciples teach others to obey King Jesus. Knowing the Bible is important; but doing what the Bible says is imperative. Mature disciples are obedient.

Third, a mature disciple is **fruitful for Jesus**. Fruitfulness is rooted in the quality of life that Christians are to display. Paul calls these the fruit of the Spirit (Galatians 5:22-23). This fruitfulness is measured by the public reputation of the disciple. Church shepherds are expected to be men who are above reproach, who are well thought of by outsiders (1 Timothy 3:1-7). Mature disciples have good reputations, both inside and outside the church. Fruitful disciples influence others to become disciples by being good neighbors, helping people solve problems, and providing comfort and care in times of need. Fruitful disciples influence others to think better about Jesus, opening the possibilities for further spiritual conversation. I like how Bobby Harrington of Discipleship.org explains this, *we are constantly loving, inviting, and encouraging those who do not follow Jesus to join us and enter this life changing relationship with God.* Mature disciples produce good fruit.

How People Mature

When I was a missionary in Kenya, I was deeply influenced by a former African missionary and educator named Tom Holland. Holland was known as the father of Theological Education by Extension, a way of training Christian leaders that influenced churches around the world. The concept

Holland promoted was simple, our Bible education efforts should produce mature, well-equipped disciples.

But what really stuck for me was Holland's very simple idea on how people mature. He illustrated the maturity process with this easy to remember diagram:

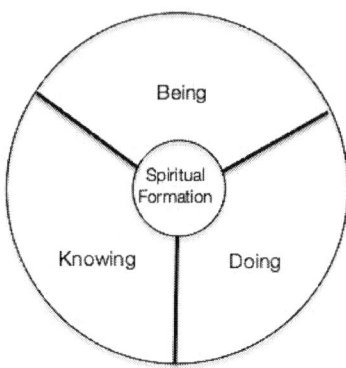

FIGURE 4. HOLLAND'S FORMATION WHEEL.

Holland said that people mature in the intersection of Knowing, Doing and Being. Being is our goal. We want Christians to **be** mature followers of Jesus, well-equipped to practice their faith across a lifetime. But Being isn't influenced directly. Being is formed indirectly through a process of reflection on information (Knowing) and experience (Doing). When Knowing and Doing are processed by reflection, people grow in their Being. This process occurs like an always-turning wheel.

The challenge we face in our church education programs is they typically focus only on Knowing. Think about what happens when we gather at church. We go to a Bible class where people sit and listen to a teacher who may desperately want people to talk (reflection), but the talk seldom gets below the surface level. Then we go and sit to listen to a sermon. Then we go home. Our "hope" is that people will do something with what they have heard (I want to use learn, but that's probably not what happened), then by some chance to take some time to reflect on it. Occasionally this does happen, but when it does it's kind of a happy accident.

I had another professor, Ed Matthews, at Abilene Christian University who gave us missionaries in training some very usable ideas on the Know, Do, Be learning cycle that I found useful in training church planters with Kairos Church Planting. As we worked to help men and women launch out to do something they had never done before we noticed they would make three statements again and again.

1. **I don't know what to do**. This is the beginning point. Before people can begin to do anything, they must know what it is they need to do. This is what the Bible class setting is best suited for, giving out information. But it's hard to do much more than give information in a Bible class. If you want your people to mature as disciples, you must provide them more than Bible classes and sermons that give them information.

2. **I don't know how to do it**. This statement is about application. It's about skill. This is when people need to see and to experience. They need to try it out so they can figure out how to do it. Doing is about training. It takes longer to learn how to do something than it does to know about something.

3. **I don't want to do it**. This statement is about motivation. This is when the being aspect comes into play. For the Christian, this is where we decide what the lordship of Jesus means to us. This is the rich young ruler who knew what to do (he'd been taught since his youth), he knew how to do it (he'd done it all his life), but when Jesus told him to sell his possessions and follow him, he went away sad (Matthew 19:21). It's at this point of being when reflection comes into play. People are figuring out the costs and the implications. They're looking at their lives to realize how they will need to change. They're making decisions about their lives that may change the direction they're heading. When we work at the being level we're working deep in the lives of people.

I want to redraw Holland's Formation Wheel for you. This time the wheel reflects the actual amount of time most churches give to each part. This is how we typically structure our discipleship formation. The greatest amount of our time and energy is spent on knowledge giving. There is some emphasis on Doing with only a sliver of attention given to the Being portion of spiritual formation.

FIGURE 5. ACTUAL FORMATION WHEEL.

I hope the difference is striking to you. The reason we spend so much more time on Knowing over Doing and Being is that Knowing is so much easier to do. It's easy to dispense information. It's easy to lay the ideas out there and then hope our people do the heavy lifting on their own. My experience is most people don't do the hard work of doing and reflecting that changes their being.

If we're going to help our people grow and mature as disciples across a lifetime, we need to restructure both our church activities and our expectations. That's what we'll look at in the next section.

House Churches, Discipleship Groups and Missional Communities

Church is a place where people need to be nurtured to live a life of faith across a lifetime. That's quite a demanding task. It's daunting to think of how we, as leaders, are to provide a way for adults to live as Jesus followers through all the changes and challenges of life.

What has characterized Christianity from its inception is that the life of faith is best experienced in relationship with fellow believers. In the first expression of the church in Jerusalem we see the church had corporate gatherings for teaching and encouragement at the Jerusalem temple. It also had more relational gatherings in smaller groups of families in their personal homes (Acts 2:46). People desire both big corporate gatherings and the opportunity of intimate friendship with fellow believers.

It seems like church in the last century did a pretty good job of naturally forming groups of members who shared life together. I look at my parents. They were part of a group of four families who truly shared their lives together for over forty years. Perhaps the less intense, fewer activity options, more integrated life of the 20th century made this an easier, more natural, option for people. But today, it seems hard to do.

Many churches have had small groups for years. If your church has a small group structure in place—well done. Don't try to make big changes in it; accentuate it. Encourage your church members to belong to one of your groups or create more groups.

There is so much good material available today on groups. Do an Amazon search for small groups, discipleship groups or missional communities and you will find any number of good books. Some authors I recommend are Alex Absalom, Mike Breen, Robby Gallaty and my friends at Discipleship.org. Each one of these authors has a particular take on groups that distinguishes the different type of groups.

House churches are very similar to the concept of small groups. House churches consist of three to ten families who serve as a relationship base. Fellowship is usually the primary focus of house churches. The house church is a place where children play while adults visit, where a meal might be shared together followed by some time of prayer, Bible study and singing. House churches are typically open for new participants and open-ended in terms of time. Some may last for years. I've known several house churches that had three different names (life groups, small groups, brothers' keepers) over twenty-five or more years, but they were always of the house church style.

Discipleship groups are more focused than house churches. Where house churches tend to be whole families, discipleship groups are usually gender specific. Their focus is typically personal accountability to living well and growing in the Word. Accountability questions and in-depth Bible study are hallmarks of discipleship groups. These groups also tend to last for a specified season, maybe six months or a year. Once they start the membership is usually closed until a new group forms.

Missional communities are similar to house churches, but larger and more specifically focused. "A missional community is an extended family of relationships, centered around Jesus, who go and make disciples amongst a specific group of people (Absalom, 2021)." Missional communities are mid-size groups of twenty-five to fifty people. Missional communities are also formed around a distinct mission. That mission may be to a neighborhood or community, a place (like a school), or serving a specific population (families with special needs children, homeless, women's abuse centers and such like). Like house churches, missional communities are multi-generational, family oriented, and may last a long time. Like discipleship groups, they have a strong, central purpose, serving a group of people and sharing Jesus with them (Breen & Absalom, *Launching Missional Communities*, 2015).

If you are trying to bring renewal to your church, you need to think about how to structure your church meeting schedule to include some type of house church in it. If you have a traditional church meeting schedule of Sunday mornings, Sunday evenings and Wednesday evenings, I would ask you the Dr. Phil question, "How's that working for you?" Few churches can sustain the three church meetings a week schedule. How can you integrate a house church style gathering into either your Sunday evenings or Wednesday evenings?

The house church gathering can be very simple. Here are four components to include.

1. **Fresh Bread**. This is feeding from the word of God. Many people find the Discovery Bible Study (DBS) a simple, powerful way to bring God's word afresh to people. DBS is centered around medium length pieces of scripture, anywhere from ten to thirty verses or so. This is not a teaching time that someone must spend time to prepare. This is a time for the group to hear God for themselves and talk about what they are hearing. Here's what you do:

a. *Read-Reread-Retell.* Someone reads the scriptures from their Bible followed by someone who reads the same passage from a different version. Then a third person retells what has been said in his or her own words (be sure this person knows before any reading starts). Then the group works through the following four questions together.

b. *God Is* . . . What do we learn about God from this passage?

c. *We are* . . . What do we learn about people from this passage?

d. *I will* . . . How will I put this passage into practice?

e. *Someone* . . . Who do I know who needs to hear this message?

2. **Shared Meals**. Table fellowship is like a healing salve. It calms people down. It gives people something to do that breaks awkwardness. Eating together is the best group ice breaker ever. Eating together promotes the practice of hospitality. And besides all that, you get to sample delicious food—together!

3. **Mutual Care**. Life can be a rough road. When people gather in your house church, they come with such a variety of experiences from the day, emotions they are feeling, hurts that need healing, confusion that needs clarifying, joys that deserve sharing, and losses that require grieving. Mealtime will surface some, but to have specific time of sharing for prayer unleashes the power of God to work.

4. **Missional Eyes**. We want to learn to see the world as God sees it. We want to notice when God works. We want to see behind all the closed doors and drawn shades into the lives of people. When we see the needs, we want to be part of ministering to those needs. Be on the lookout for opportunities for your house church to serve others as a group. Plan a serving opportunity for your group at least quarterly.

Of the three essential activities of revitalizing a church—evangelizing, serving and disciple making—it is probably discipling that is the least formed.

Two resources I recommend to you are Discipleship.org and the *Disciple Maker's Handbook*. At Discipleship.org you have access to a variety of helpful materials on disciple making. The *Disciple Maker's Handbook* is a guided, in-depth study of disciple making with practical exercises for maturing disciples.

Reflection Questions

1. What are the activities or programs your church uses to mature disciples?

2. What criteria does your church use to measure the growth or maturity of your disciples?

3. What is one idea this chapter raised for you that your church could implement in its role in making disciples?

Scripture Study

Matthew 28:18-20

- What are the two descriptions Jesus says about himself? Why is that important to discipleship?

    1. _____

    2. _____

- Jesus tells us four actions we should take as part of his disciple making mission, list these here:

    Therefore _____ *and* _____ *of*

    all nations, _____ *them in the name of the*

Father and of the Son and of the Holy Spirit, and _____ *them to obey everything I have commanded you.*

- Which of these activities have the disciples in your church traditionally done best and which is most underrepresented among your church's disciples?

PART 4 – CLOSING WELL

"Churches have a lifespan about the length of a normal human being."

This is such an insightful statement. As you've read through this book, I hope the idea of a typical lifespan of a church has been normalized for you. Churches tend to be planted generationally. Generations have preferences, expectations, and callings that are somewhat unique to their space and time. A generation starts churches that address their unique situations. These churches often last through the founders' generation to their children and grandchildren. By the time the founders are passing on, the situations that called those churches into being have also passed on and those churches no longer meet the needs or the challenges of the world around them. Those once thriving churches lose their energy and their relevance and soon, they pass on too. This is the normal lifecycle of a church.

However, we have also seen that because churches are collections of people, they have the opportunity to renew themselves, to extend their lifespan well beyond the normal range of an individual's life. To do that the church must remake itself. It must gain a new mission and vision and be filled with new people who bring renewed vitality, energy, and resources with them. This is the undeniable key. New people bring new life with them. Reaching new people with the gospel is God's evergreen plan for healthy life for his church on earth.

In the preceding section we looked at the three essential activities a church must accomplish for revitalization: 1) evangelizing, 2) serving, and 3) discipling. In this final section we'll turn our focus to the idea of closing. Or perhaps a more useful term might be transitioning. It might not be time for your church to close, but you may need to transition out of where you are to another situation that is more helpful to your people—and to God's kingdom.

CHAPTER 10 – CREATE AN ESTATE PLAN

You can view a video of this chapter at Heritage21.org by creating a personal account and enrolling into the H21 course: *About My Church's Future*.

What is Estate Planning?

What is estate planning for churches? When an individual creates an estate plan it includes more than a last will and testament that directs who gets what. The process usually involves a competent attorney who helps the client understand the process and the decisions they need to make. It includes financial planning for the client's future, how to avoid unnecessary costs, taking stock of how God has blessed the client financially and how the client can bless others after death. In other words, good estate planning is good stewardship.

As we have seen, research shows that most churches have a typical lifespan of sixty to maybe one hundred years, about the lifespan of a person. Since churches often have estates—land, buildings, and furnishings that have financial value—comprehensive planning for the future is as valid for churches as it is for individuals. Church estate planning recognizes the need for every church to think about the following conditions:

1. Planning for the unforeseen, circumstances like shifts in neighborhood demographics, aging membership, and economic disruption.

2. How to preserve and extend the mission of the church to take the gospel to all the world. This often is part of legacy creation for the church.

3. How to protect and ensure your church's fiscal resources are used for God's purposes. How do you think beyond today and beyond yourselves, to use your congregational resources appropriately and effectively for God's work?

4. And finally, to prepare for the eventuality that your church will someday reach the end of its natural lifespan. This happens to churches in rural communities. It happens in suburbs. It happens in large cities.

In other words, church estate planning is good stewardship of the mission and resources of the church. The Heritage 21 Foundation believes every church needs to pay attention to estate planning. At minimum, this entails reviewing its Articles of Incorporation and Church By-Laws. This can be done quickly and easily as part of the church's ongoing vision renewal every three to five years. Older churches need to add to this a review of the church estate, church health, and how the church might apportion its estate giving in the future.

Unfortunately, it's our experience that very few churches have given much thought to estate planning or preparation beyond, perhaps, preparing their annual budget.

Elements of Church Estate Planning

What are the elements of a comprehensive estate plan for your church? There are many, but here are several issues that many churches do not seem to be addressing which good stewardship demands.

Decision-Making
Do you have a usable decision-making process that involves your members, allows for a variety of perspectives to be heard, and that works gently toward consensus building while allowing room for differences? Every church needs a decision-making process that's biblically oriented, that's not stifled by lowest common denominator thinking, that's forward looking, mission centric, and outward focused.

Our observation is that often church leaders, particularly those of smaller congregations, are often plagued by these conditions:

- Their primary attention is given to what their members want (often expressed by who complains).
- They are overly sensitive to risk avoidance.

- They group too many decisions under the heading of theological practice.

If you have a good decision-making process, one that is well thought out, you have a roadmap to follow that will keep you out of the ditch, so to speak. If you don't have a good decision-making process, you may find yourself being held hostage by a dominant personality or even by a gentle soul whom no one wants to hurt. Either type of person can keep you from making the decisions your church needs to make. A good decision-making process may help you avoid an impasse that leaves your church stuck and frustrated in an unhealthy situation.

Legal Issues

A second area of estate planning for churches are legal issues, particularly those that define your membership and protect your physical resources. Watch our video, *Legal stewardship and the church* for a full presentation on legal issues.

Churches are permitted by state law to exist as legal corporate entities. If they are not incorporated, they are an unincorporated association, which subjects all the members to potential legal and financial liability. To operate legally, a church must be registered in its state through filing Articles of Incorporation with the Secretary of State, and operating according to its By-Laws. These are very important documents, affecting the legal corporate operation of the church, protecting the church assets, and protecting the members from legal liability. Most often, these documents were created at the time the congregation was formed, often without appropriate consideration of the uniqueness of autonomous congregations. When we ask congregations about their Articles of Incorporation and By-Laws, they often have no idea where these documents reside or what they say.

Because these documents may be fifty years old or older, they may have restrictions, language or directions which are no longer applicable or desired. The Articles of Incorporation may not insure the property is legally identified and appropriately devoted to Kingdom use within our fellowship. The By-Laws may have outdated expectations on how the leadership of the congregation is to be structured. There is a strong possibility the By-Laws do not have a good way to determine who is a voting member, how congregation-wide decisions are to be formalized, and the processes for buying, selling, and holding title to real estate. Without knowing it, a church can lose its status as a protected corporation simply by failing to operate as a corporation or not filing the annual reports required by some states.

When was the last time you reviewed your corporate documents? How would you assess your church's legal status and risk profile? The Heritage 21 Foundation can provide you with sample legal documents that can be tailored to your congregation's needs and circumstances, or the Foundation will consult with your legal advisors to review your legal status and revise your legal documents as appropriate.

Church Real Estate
What is the status of your church's real estate titles and stewardship expectations of its property? Have you looked lately to see what happens to your property if your church should decline and close? Most standardized legal forms just provide that it's to be distributed to another nonprofit organization. Is that what you think the many members who have sacrificially given to your church over the years would want to happen to those resources? And what about the need for protections against takeover scams? Unfortunately, we know firsthand of churches that have lost their real estate to individual families or outside religious groups who do not share their commitment to scripture. And there are hundreds, maybe even thousands, of congregations whose property is deteriorating. Again, is that the kind of stewardship you want to present to God and to the people around you? Again, for further information watch our video: *What You Should Know About Stewardship of your Church Real Estate*.

Risk Management
Every congregation has a risk profile. We are, after all, public entities whose business is people. Church leaders should be both aware of potential risks and should address them periodically. Often it seems that the proposed cure-all is to have an adequate insurance policy. And that's certainly important. But there are other risks that should be regularly reviewed by the leadership. These risks may include practices revolving around: hiring and supervising staff, financial and accounting practices, conflicts of interest, safety management, and officer and employee behavior and practices.

Financial Redistribution

Any estate that includes financial resources needs a plan to distribute those resources. At Heritage 21 we call this "repurposing." Repurposing is taking financial resources and blessings that God has already provided in one place and repurposing them for better use locally or someplace else. Another way to look at financial redistribution is as legacy creation. When a church closes, it can bless hundreds and thousands of other people by investing in new churches and ministries that will touch people they, as a church, would never otherwise be able to touch.

As part of creating an estate plan, ask yourself this question, "If we were to close tomorrow and sell our property, how would we like that money to be used?" We suggest something like this very simple formula (percentages are provided for illustration).

1. Designate 25% to planting new churches that will carry on the legacy of your church. The Heritage 21 Foundation can help you do this.
2. Give 25% to a missionary work somewhere in the world.
3. Give the remaining 50% to 3 ministries, schools, camps, etc. that your congregation would like to bless.

Challenges to Healthy Church Estate Planning

What are some of the challenges to conducting a healthy church estate planning process? Here are a number of items for you to think about to help you conduct a healthy and productive church estate planning process. Once a church begins a downward spiral, it takes great courage and perseverance to overcome these obstacles, which include:

1. A controlling leadership instead of a nurturing, open leadership.
2. An aged church body that lacks the energy, vision, or resources to plan and work towards a bright future.
3. A general lack of leadership.
4. Inability to resolve internal conflict in a healthy and God honoring manner.

5. Insistence on doing everything like you've always done it. Which, as you know, will result in more of what you've got.
6. Resistance to professional assistance from outside help for congregational planning, legal advice and/or real estate issues.
7. Failure to consider new ideas or the leading of the Holy Spirit.
8. Insufficient financial resources to maintain facilities, much less reach out to a lost and hurting world.
9. Rapidly changing demographics of the congregation or the community.
10. An inward focus versus an outward, outreach orientation.
11. An unwillingness to acknowledge that the church's lifecycle may be nearing its end, coupled with a hesitancy to make any decisions about the church's future.

Our experience is that if THREE OR MORE of the above obstacles are present in your congregation, your church most likely needs to re-evaluate your future to make the best kingdom stewardship decisions you can. And again, most likely you will need outside help for planning, legal advice, and real estate issues.

Considering the current rapid decline in membership and attendance among many congregations, we strongly encourage you to invest important time reviewing your church's estate plan or creating one if you do not currently have one. The Heritage 21 Foundation is posting helpful information and contracts on our web site at Heritage21.org. We recommend first that your leadership review together the material in this booklet. Make a list of the specific needs with which you might need help. Watch the videos *About Your Church's Future* on the Heritage 21 website for further insights. We are here to help you with resources, expertise, and encouragement.

Reflection Questions

1. Where are your legal documents and have you reviewed then in the last 3 years? Find your church's Articles of Incorporation and By-

Laws. What changes or revisions might serve you better than what is currently in them?

2. Go ahead and make your own personal distribution list. Where would you like to see your church bless God's kingdom if your church were to close today?

3. Look over the challenges to healthy church estate planning. Which of these describe your church?

Scripture Study

Luke 16:1-15

- In this story, what can you say about this steward's position and performance?

- What happened when the steward was called to account for his actions?

- Good stewards use material resources to influence people in spiritual ways. How might God expect churches to use their material resources to influence people for God's kingdom?

- How might God hold accountable a church that fails to steward its resources well for his kingdom's sake?

CHAPTER 11 – TIMELINE AND ESSENTIAL MARKERS

I know the thought of closing the doors of your church is a difficult one. We've talked to enough leaders who have been unable to go there. Remember those leader responses we talked about in chapter 9? *Not on my watch* is one of the big, emotional responses leaders feel. You don't want to come out of this feeling like you've failed. What if you can give this one more try?

That's what this book is ultimately about—giving it one more try. Everything we have covered is intended to help you face realities so you can make a plan and move forward. In this chapter we'll put all the ideas we've talked about into a general revitalization plan. Understand, every church is unique, so you will need to adapt this general plan into a specific plan for your church. That's where Heritage 21 Foundation encourages you to get outside help from someone who has the ability and experience to coach you. We can put you in touch with a good church coach.

Hiring a coach is one of the best ways to raise your chances for successfully moving towards a new future. A good coach will help you in three critical areas:

1. A coach will help you develop an appropriate plan for your church. Churches are notoriously inexperienced at planning. Most churches expect to run on auto pilot, to do the same things in the same ways. Remember, in this new reality a church needs to rethink and replan about every three years!

2. A coach will keep you accountable for doing the things you've said you will do. If churches are bad at planning, they are even worse at implementation! Churches are largely volunteer organizations. That means almost anything that comes along in the life of the volunteer elder, deacon, ministry leader, Bible class teacher, small group leader, etc. is liable to take precedence over the needs of the church. This means that even good plans lose traction and soon, in three or four months, they fall by the wayside and the status quo returns to

normal. A coach will hold you responsible to do what you've agreed to do when you need to do it.

3. A coach will help you find the resources you need to do what needs to be done. No one today has all the answers to all the challenges we face in our churches. But a good coach will have contact with more people and more resources than you are likely to know. You're hiring a coach to be a resource finder for you! Your coach will commit time and effort to find potential answers to your challenges.

Now, let's get to that plan.

Create Your Plan

"If it's in your head, it's only an idea. You don't have a plan until it is written." This is an axiom I used with church planters for years. But it's an idea I have seen in my life. In our early parenting years my wife and I would go away for our anniversary. Besides going for the enjoyment of being together, we also used this time to reflect on our past year and talk about what we would like to see in the coming year. We'd write down those ideas and put them into our anniversary folder. When we got home, we'd put the folder back into the file cabinet and usually not look at it again until the next anniversary. But you know what? A year later we were always amazed at how many of those ideas and dreams we wrote down had happened! There is something powerful about putting ideas into writing. That's why you need a written plan.

If you've been in a profession where planning is essential, you've probably used a Gantt chart. A Gantt chart is a tool that displays the tasks or activities to be done and the time that they are expected to take. What the Gantt chart does is give you a visual representation of your plan. Below is a visual of the general 18-month plan I'll walk you through here:

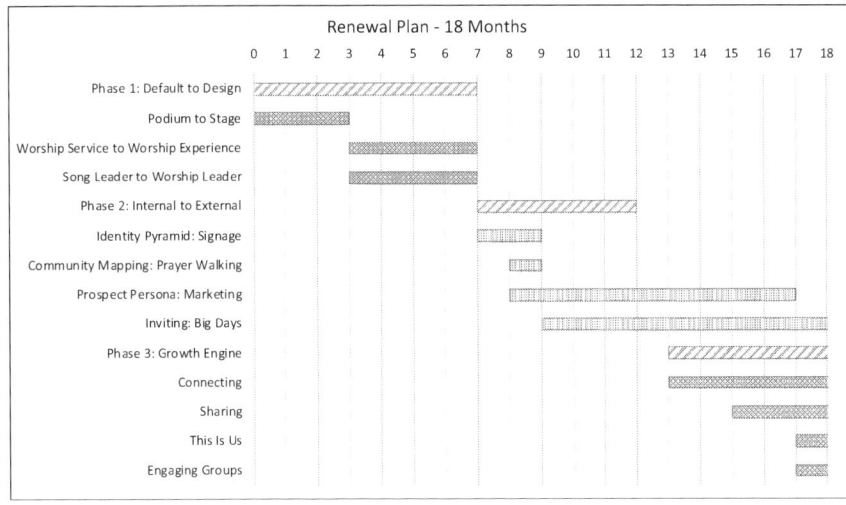

This plan has three phases that you will focus on for s months each.

- Phase 1 Default to Design
- Phase 2: Internal to External
- Phase 3: Growth Engine

In each phase there are specific activities or actions to work on. Each action has a measurable item that you will need to define so you know when you accomplish it. Also, don't just think of these as something only to accomplish. You will learn new skills, new habits, and new ways of thinking. Along the way, these activities will help you develop the new skills, habits, and ways of thinking you need to successfully renew.

Default to Design

I've mentioned several times that most churches exist on maintenance mode. For most elders, as long as everything stays the same and the boat doesn't rock everything is good. That won't work anymore, you're going to have to let go that emotional life ring. That means you're going to need to reshape your thinking from *Default*, doing what we've always done, to *Design*, doing what needs to be done to be a healthy church.

There are many things that could be done here. But the three shifts we'll focus on have to do with the worship gathering. The reason is, if you are going to renew, you need to be able to attract, gather and retain new people. If the way you are currently doing church isn't doing this—you must learn how to attract and retain new people. These shifts are designed to help you learn these critical changes.

The pre-step to this change is good communication. You can't just decide to do these then spring it on the church one Sunday. You need to prepare your church. Talk about what your church is facing. Let people express their fears, concerns, and anxieties. Explain what you're thinking and why. Describe what will happen and the results you are praying to see. Be consistently open with your people.

Podium to Stage
What do people see and expect when they walk into your auditorium? I would guess that they see the same thing every week—and they've been seeing it for years. You see, what most churches do is build a podium—that's the big platform where the preacher stands. He stands on the podium, behind a lectern, where he can keep his notes. Maybe the baptistry is behind him covered by an aging, neutral color curtain. There might be a deacon's bench to one side, and maybe a flower arrangement or potted trees or two. In front of the podium is the Lord's Supper table with *This Do In Remembrance of Me* inscribed on the front.

There is nothing wrong with any of these things. But there is a problem, a communication problem. When people walk into your auditorium, they walk into an area they have learned to ignore. There is no place for expectation, no cues to create anticipation. In a not so gentle word that a child would use—it's boring!

In your first three months your goal is to turn your podium into a stage. A stage is where action happens. A stage speaks; it communicates. A stage is dynamic. It gives hints and clues to people that something is going to happen.

One of the best uses of a church stage I have experienced was at a church in Portland, Oregon. The church was beginning a three-month study of the book of Romans. On their stage they had laid out a chain link fence for a background. Around the stage they had scattered some old tires, wooden pallets and other odds and ends. It looked a mess! But as their preacher progressed through the sermon series the stage changed until finally it was a beautiful representation of a park! Their stage transformed week by week before our eyes. Isn't that the ultimate message of Romans? *Be transformed by the renewing of your mind* (Romans 12:2). They used their stage to communicate the gospel. Each week people came wondering, "What has changed today?" Their sense of anticipation was palpable.

I hope you can tell that while the Gantt chart has you working on this podium to stage shift the first three months, this is not a one and done activity. Keeping a good stage takes planning. It takes your preacher planning important worship series with a certain rhythm across the year. You can also fold in seasons and holidays onto your stage. It will take practice and require work to keep your stage communicating well. Start small, be consistent, and be intentional as you move from podium to stage.

Worship Service to Worship Experience
As you work on your move from podium to stage you should begin to develop a different mindset. That's what this next item is about. The second shift is from a worship service to a worship experience.

Think about people today. What services do they go to? If you ask almost anyone their first answer is likely to be a funeral service! People go to funerals, but they're not high on the "want to" list. Unfortunately, that's how most people who are not Christians feel about church services. A church service is something they avoid. Your task to learn how to create an experience that people will enjoy and want to be at.

This is something that is not easy to describe but you know it when you experience it. It doesn't take a lot of fancy to do it either. The Renovatus Church in Vancouver, Washington was and remains a smaller church with fewer than one hundred people. But every time I worshipped with them it was an experience where I anticipated the presence of God. They had learned to let God appear and follow His lead. And you know what? When God appears, lives change.

When people find your worship life-giving, full of the presence of God, you won't be able to keep them away.

Song Leader to Worship Leader
I grew up with that single song leader who stood in front of us with his songbook in hand, announcing the song number to us (with the song numbers posted on the wooden signboard), then saying, "All found, let us sing." That was a great experience for me. The problem is that doesn't work today. When is the last time you saw someone on TV announce their song and beat out a time signature? Never! A song leader leads songs, a worship leader calls us into the throne room of God.

Our fellowship has struggled to raise worship leaders. It is much easier to pick out a half dozen songs then to help open the windows of heaven. One option churches have used to help their worship is a worship team. This team is three to five people who will talk about, pray about, and plan the worship together. Let them dream about what God is wanting to do over the next few months. They are going to be your team that listens to God and to your people, whose great joy will be seeing the two meet.

Does this also mean you will have a worship team on stage? Not necessarily, churches have often given their worship teams microphones in their seats. It is my opinion that having a worship team visible on the stage benefits the overall worship experience both live and on video. But start first with a planning team and then gradually up the worship team's presence if you can.

Internal to External

Phase 2 moves the church from an *Internal* focus to an *External* focus. In this day and age, when we are struggling and hoping that people will return to church, there is even more reason to put your focus on those people who are outside your walls, those who aren't with you regularly—or at all.

Identity Pyramid: Signage
The first activity I suggest to help churches make this shift is to coach them through creating their identity pyramid. The identity pyramid starts with Basic Biblical Beliefs as a foundation, then builds the pyramid with values,

mission, vision, focus people, strategies, activities, and the people who lead those activities.

While it sounds simple, this is usually a full weekend coaching event for a church. What the Identity Pyramid does is reveal the heart of the church. It answers the question, "Who are we?"

The outcome we look for, besides the pyramid, is creating signage around and within the church that begins to reflect the heart of the church. It is so easy to overlook the power of signage that helps orient and direct people when they visit with you. When you think of signage you must think about the people who have yet to visit you, but who will. This begins your focus on those external to your church.

Community Mapping: Prayer Walking
We have gone through the time when the big, mega churches were a norm. Yes, the mega church is likely to stay with us. But the more local, community-oriented churches seem to be making a comeback. For me, these smaller churches who embed themselves in their communities are what I hope and expect to see.

If you're going to connect with your community, you need to know your community. That is the purpose of prayer walking your community. The process of prayer walking begins with a map where you can see your church in the midst of your community. Then identify the boundaries around your church. What are the big roads, major intersections, public buildings, other churches, etc. What kind of people live in your community? What is their age and stage of life, their education, their work? Where are the single-family areas and the multi-family zones? Where do people shop, play, and seek entertainment? All these things are part of knowing your community.

Ultimately, you will get your church people onto the streets with a map of the streets they should walk through. Give them some specific items to look for and specifics to pray about. When your people are done, debrief them about what they saw, who they met, and the intuitions they gained about your community. Above all, keep your eye out for where God is at work in your community or where he needs to be at work, and how you might join Him.

Focus People: Marketing

Marketing—is that a dirty word for churches? Absolutely not! Here is the approved definition for marketing of the American Marketing Association: *Marketing is . . . creating, communicating, delivering, and exchanging offerings that have **value** for customers, clients, partners, and society at large.* At its core, marketing is how an entity offers value to others. Yet most churches pay very little attention to marketing. I've yet to work with a church that had a marketing line item in its budget.

What happens when your church does not have a marketing strategy and plan? First, you lose control over what people know about you. People in your community are going to fabricate an opinion about your church. They use anything they see (your parking lot, signs, building, the number of cars in the parking lot, the kinds of people they see) or hear about you to create a mental impression, a cubby hole, in which they put your church. Whether that picture they frame is accurate or not makes no difference, it's the picture they have. Marketing is your opportunity to create the kind of picture in their minds that you want them to have of you.

Second, you lose the opportunity to become an option in their life. Missionaries are usually knowledgeable about the concept of receptivity. Receptivity is the intensity of the readiness and willingness people have to consider Jesus. Receptivity among Americans is at a low ebb. Culturally, Christians are assumed to be anti-progress. Perceptions of Christians often include only negative positions—stands against abortion, same sex marriage, and women in high offices—items of cultural value today. This sense of Christianity as being so out of touch with modern life is so strong among non-believers that, for many, church is the very last place they would go for care, comfort, or understanding. It is through intentional, active marketing of what we stand for that you have the opportunity to become a valid option for people in your community to explore.

The starting point of marketing is knowing the people whom you are most likely to connect with. These become your mission focus people. Saddleback church quite famously created *Saddleback Sam* as a way to visualize the people their church was built to connect with. A general way to describe your focus people is to create a visualized description, a word portrait. The

Mission Focus People is your understanding of the people you will intentionally love, serve, and share Jesus with.

Here's an example of a mission focus people description that Kairos Church Planting developed to focus on young people who would be good candidates for an apprenticeship with a church planter:

FIGURE 6. MISSION FOCUS PEOPLE.

When I coach with a church, we work together to create a description like this one that will guide the church in their marketing. Often, we will use a picture of a real person already in the congregation who reflects their focus people. That puts flesh and blood to the idea.

With your focus people in mind, we then look at what people see when they drive by the church, when they run across the church website, and when the church is out in the community. Then we begin to investigate how to create the kind of message that this person will be willing to listen to in the first 3 seconds or at a glance. Eventually you might work with a graphic designer who will help coordinate the kinds of printed and electronic materials your church will distribute.

Inviting: Big Days

Fifty years ago, Big Days happened in the context of gospel meetings, times when the church put on a big push to invite family, friends, co-workers, and neighbors to church to hear the traveling preacher. Fifteen years ago, a Big Day was something like a Friend's and Neighbors Day at church, a time when the church would have a special service, maybe with a potluck afterwards. This Big Day was usually connected to a new sermon series that people might be interested in.

Today, the Big Day idea is morphing again. I don't think we have sufficient evidence to define what it will be, but my guess is its leaning towards events that allow people to build relationships with others. A Big Day may be a play day at the park, a service day at a homeless shelter, a backyard BBQ, a coffee house poetry reading night or any number of events that can act as a Point of Entry event (Benevon.com).

There are two keys to a Big Day event. First, it gives your people a reason to become inviters. Personal invitation remains the single most potent tool for connecting your church with new people. Second, the Big Day event will help build your database. We'll look at the database a bit deeper in the following section. What the Big Day does is it puts you in talking range of people whom you can influence towards Jesus.

Growth Engine

Every church has a growth engine. Sometimes, though, that engine has quit functioning. A church growth engine has four cylinders to it, as seen in the illustration below: 1) Worship, 2) Service, 3) Groups and 4) Sharing Faith.

Growth engine

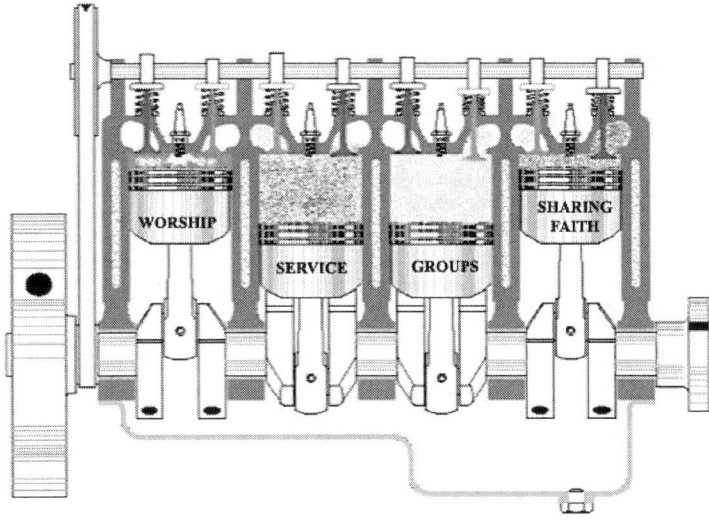

FIGURE 7. CHURCH GROWTH ENGINE.

A healthy church might do two of these four cylinders well and minimally address the other two. The goal of a renewing church is to get one cylinder working well and a second cylinder that is developing. Since a renewing church is already having worship gatherings, that is the one to start on developing. That's why the Default to Design phase focuses on worship items. New churches will typically start by developing their service cylinder because that is a natural way they have of connecting with new people.

In the growth engine phase, there are four key items that need to be developed.

Connecting

How do you know new people? That seems a strange question, but if you're going to renew or grow you need to begin to know more new people, a lot of new people. One way to answer this question is by numbers. In new church plants, if they want to do well, they need to gather a database of 1,000 people in their first year.

The second way to answer this question is by your ability to remember and contact those 1,000 new people. The only effective way to do this is through a database. That database can be as simple as a spreadsheet or as complex as cloud-based church management system. If you already are using church management software like Fellowship One, Tithe.ly, Church Community Builder, or Realm—good for you. That's your starting point. If you are not, you can always start with something like Excel or Google Sheets and grow from there.

The database is where you will collect at least two pieces of information: 1) first and last names and 2) at least one way of contacting (cell phone number is the best, followed by email). Now you have a way to begin to share events and ideas that are meaningful to these people, and you can begin to track their interest and involvement.

Many times, churches shy away from something so inane as a database. But I argue that if you don't know someone's name and how to contact them, you must not love them very much. A church database is a creation of love and a desire for people to know Jesus.

Sharing
How do you know that people who come to your church will have a valid opportunity to consider Jesus as Lord and Savior of their life? Well of course they can—can't they? Don't people hear that in our sermons? Today it takes about two years for a person to make the journey from unbelief to faith in Jesus expressed in baptism. There's a whole heap of question asking, doubt overcoming, and trying things out involved in helping people believe in Jesus today. In fact, most people who make that journey of unbelief to belief go through two conversions. The first conversion is the willingness to accept that Jesus and Christianity have any value. The second conversion is the decision to be a Christ follower or not.

While sermons and your worship gatherings do help this journey, the best way is for people to be involved in a group with other people who are also in that journey. Since I was a deacon at the Vancouver Church of Christ in Vancouver, Washington I have used the Alpha Course as that place where people can meet Jesus and make a valid decision about their second conversion.

The Alpha Course is an eleven-week, small group experience that allows people to make friends and ask questions in a non-threatening environment. There's no magic to Alpha. But the fact that it is so well packaged and so broadly used makes it as easy a program to offer as anything available. The Alpha Course assures you that you have an ongoing, repeatable place where people will encounter Jesus and be able to decide if they want to become Jesus followers.

This Is Us
The TV show *This Is Us* has attracted a huge fan base because it brings us into the lives of its characters. We get to see them manage life and meet its challenges. We learn who they are. That's the idea of creating a *This Is Us* activity. Sometimes these are called 101 classes, Meet the Minister, or any number of names. What you are creating is a space where people who are considering your church can learn what you believe, how you act, what your mission is and how they can connect with that mission. It is also a time when they can be introduced to ways they can be involved. These events can be as short as a two-hour activity following worship to a four-week class.

Engaging Groups
The Natural Church Development (NCD) survey measures Eight Quality Characteristics that characterize healthy churches. One of these characteristics is Holistic Small Groups. NCD has recognized via worldwide research that people need small group connections to thrive in their spiritual lives, to help them feel connected and needed, and to be centers for disciple-making. Small groups are a place of belonging that knit people together. Small groups are also great places for stickiness. New people are far more likely to stick to a church through the relationship building context of a small group than they are the more anonymous context of a worship service. For years now people have asked about the secret sauce to a small group. If there is one, my vote is eating together.

Identify Your Essential Measures

You don't pursue the activities and items described above just to do them. You do those things so you can reach new people. Connecting new people to your is the only remedy for decline. The only way you will know if you are making progress is if you have something to measure.

At the beginning of a renewal process a good coach will help you identify your goals. Here are four areas of goal setting.

1. **New connections** – You won't grow much if you wait for people to stumble into your building. You need to be seeking them. You measure new connections by the number of new people you add to your database. In a renewal process, your church should aim for 250 new connections in the first six months. By the end of eighteen months the goal should be a database of 1,000 people whom you know by name and can contact at any time.

2. **Visitors** – For renewal churches the two primary arenas for visitors should be in your worship gatherings and your service events. These are the areas where it is easiest to invite people to be involved. A goal for a renewing church is to have 200 visitors in the first eighteen months. A visitor is a first-time guest to your church and who has agreed to let you add their name and contact information to your database. This agreement can be as simple as completing a contact card.

3. **Baptisms** – For years the average church has tended to have one baptism for every eighty attenders. If you are a church of fifty people that won't cut it. The goal for baptisms in the first eighteen months should be eight. Eight baptisms will typically bring five new families with typically four people per family for a total of twenty new members. Those twenty new members will push you over the survivability threshold.

4. Internal energy – This is measuring how much energy is in your leadership and your church to tackle a renewal process. This internal energy is measured by four items measured on a scale of 1 (lowest) to 5 (highest):

    a. Anticipation of Worship

    b. Energy for Transition

    c. Optimism for your church

    d. Invitations made to church activities in the last 6 months

The average scores for your leadership and key members should be 4 or above at the end of twelve months.

Conclusion

The purpose of this chapter is to give you an idea of a general plan for renewing your church. If it feels like a lot of work—it is. Most churches in the distress of decline hope that there is an easy answer to getting back to the way church used to be. There isn't. Our 21st century world is radically different from the 20th century world in which most churches grew and thrived.

The Heritage 21 Foundation and its partners are more than willing to help your church engage a renewal process. But before that happens, we also want you to know what you are committing to. Yes, it is a lot of hard work. It is probably work that your church has not done in a very long time. But if you will follow the plan, are willing to learn new skills, habits, and ways of thinking, we believe God will be glorified no matter what the outcome.

Reflection Questions

1. How did reading through this general revitalization plan make you feel about your church's possibility of revitalizing?

2. Which of the shifts (podium to stage, worship service to worship experience, song leader worship leader) do you think our church would most readily work on? Why?

3. What have you learned about a church growth engine? What have you learned about your church's growth engine?

Scripture Study

1 Corinthians 3:10-15

- How should we look at our church buildings and resources within the teaching of this passage?

- How might we be susceptible to a pride that unjustifiably prevents us from transitioning a small, aging group of people out of a building that is too big and too much for them?

- What kinds of activities and treasures can a church have in its history that are precious and were fruitful for God's glory?

- What message do you think this passage brings for a church that understands its best decision would be to close?

CHAPTER 12 – WHAT IF IT DOESN'T HAPPEN?

Most leaders in declining churches want to know if their church can renew. That's a great hope. At this point, I hope you realize that hope is not a plan. I'm confident that if your church were to follow the general plan laid out in the previous chapter and met the metrics that you would succeed in your renewal.

But the reality is that fewer than five percent of churches that have moved into the tanking zone of their lifecycle will in fact be able to successfully renew. Those are not very good odds. The reason for such low odds is the things that got you to the point you are at today are the same things that will prevent your renewal. It comes down to the idea that churches best serve the generation in which that church was started. By the time a church is in its third generation, the needs, the values, and the expectations of people have changed so much that the church is no longer able to serve them well. So, the church dies.

While the closing of a church is always a sad event it does not have to be a tragic event. The fact is, every movement of churches needs to see at least two percent of its churches close each year to be healthy and future oriented. When closing churches are willing to pass forward the blessings of finances and facilities to a future generation, they are distributing those blessings into the future.

In this final chapter we look at what you should do if you conclude that your best stewardship for God's kingdom is to sell your church property and transition your church to something smaller, or to stop meeting all together.

Set Your Priorities

There are two important decisions to make about your church property: 1) what to do with your building and lands and 2) how to distribute any proceeds.

There are just three options for a church to choose concerning its land and buildings.

- **Option 1:** use those resources to keep its ever-dwindling group together until those resources are used up. This feels like the evil or lazy steward who buried the single talent the rich man had given him (Matthew 25:14-30).

- **Option 2:** give the land and buildings to another non-profit group. There are some good things in option 2. There are new churches that will struggle to buy and build, but who could be blessed by receiving a building from a church that is closing. This keeps the kingdom alive and serving in that community.

  What often happens with option 2 is that these valuable resources are given to the nearest community church (or the church that is already renting the facility). When this happens the benefit to our fellowship is lost completely. We have many missionaries and church planters who desperately need support.

  If you feel like giving your resources to another church group is a good option for you, consider selling it to them at a reduced price and invest those sale proceeds into the Heritage 21 Foundation. The H21 Foundation will distribute those funds to good works from our fellowship.

- **Option 3:** give the land and buildings to a nearby congregation of Churches of Christ. Again, there are good things about option 3. You will retain the benefit of your capital of faith to encourage and help Churches of Christ. If you do this, please consider if the church you are giving your lands and buildings to will be able to steward those resources well for the expansion of the kingdom.

  We have encountered too many churches who received the lands and buildings of a closing church with all the good intentions of using them for church planting and missions. But then reality intrudes, and that money goes into paving parking lots, reroofing the building, or remodeling the bathrooms. I wish I could say I made up those options, but I didn't. Again, if you feel that giving your resources to a nearby Church of Christ is your best option would you consider investing twenty-five percent into the Heritage 21 Foundation to bless church planters and missionaries?

Deal with Real Estate Realities

I was sitting with a church elder listening to him talk about the plans their church had for renewal. They had an old building they could no longer afford to manage, but it still had a lot of worth. They were going to sell the building, replant the church, and make a significant contribution to the Heritage 21 Foundation for church planting. It was a great plan!

Then the fly got into the ointment. They had a member who was a real estate agent with whom they had signed a contract. This was done with good intentions and in good faith. But this member was a residential realtor. He had no experience and no knowledge of commercial real estate. After a year (enough time for the contract to expire) this elder came back to Heritage 21 and asked for help. It didn't take long before their building was under contract, sold, and they were on their way to replanting themselves as a new church. Later I shared coffee with this same elder who was so thankful for the help his church received from Heritage 21.

Church buildings are commercial properties. It takes a different skill set to sale a church building than it does a residential house. The Heritage 21 Foundation has board members and ambassadors who have spent their careers in commercial real estate. These men and women will help you get the best prices for your building and sell it more quickly than most people you could find locally.

Management Challenges

It's not quite as easy to close a church building as locking the doors. There are important details that need to be taken care of. Insurance must be maintained on the building until it is sold. There will still be utility costs to be paid. There are safety and security issues, garbage, and repairs that may need to be made in order to sell at the best price. There are also the decisions that must be made about the furniture, supplies, and other movable items stored inside the building.

The Heritage 21 Foundation offers you a turnkey option by creating an agreement on how your church wants to distribute the proceeds and allow Heritage 21 to manage and sale the property so you do not have to. This process is based on a working agreement that clearly identifies how you want to disburse the net income of the proceeds.

Celebrate Your Church's Life

It's also important to celebrate the life of your church. There have been some wonderful closing day worship events where past members have come to share memories together about all the good things God has done in and through "their" church.

Heritage 21 believes those memories and works of God deserve to be recorded in video and passed on to future generations. We'll bring a videographer in to do interviews and capture the precious moments of a church closing. If your church uses the Heritage 21 Foundation to distribute your funds, copies of that video will be sent to those who receive your money so they can share the good news of your church with the new people they meet and bring into God's great kingdom. It is a glorious heritage of faith that you pass on to others.

Reflection Questions

1. Given all you have read in this book, what do you think the best decision for your church is?
2. How can you share what you have learned here with other leaders in your church?

Scripture Study

1 Timothy 2:1-13

- How, at this stage in your church's life, how can your church best pass on what you have heard to "faithful men?"
- In what ways can your church please God?

- Why is Paul ready "to endure everything for the sake of the elect? What does he mean by this?

BIBLIOGRAPHY

Absalom, Alex. "Why Missional Communities?" *RSS*, https://churchinnovationlab.com/p/aboutmcs.

Barna Group. "One in Three Practicing Christians Has Stopped Attending Church during COVID-19." *Barna Group*, 8 July 2020, https://www.barna.com/research/new-sunday-morning-part-2.

Bolsinger, Todd. *Canoeing the Mountains: Christian Leadership in Uncharted Territory*. Westmont, IL: InterVarsity Press, 2018.

Breen, Mike. *Building a Discipling Culture, 3rd edition*. 3DM Publishing, 2017.

Breen, Mike and Absalom, Alex. *Launching Missional Communities*. 3DM International, 2015.

"Definitions of Marketing." *American Marketing Association*, 30 Sept. 2021, https://www.ama.org/the-definition-of-marketing-what-is-marketing.

Discovery Bible Study, https://www.dbsguide.org.

Gallaty, Robbie and Swain, Chris. *Replicate: How to Create a Culture of Disciple-Making Right Where You Are*. Chicago: Moody, 2020.

Granberg, Stanley E. *Leading Others: Sharing Faith*. Amazon, Create Space, 2015.

Grenz, Stanley J. *A Primer on Postmodernism*. Grand Rapids, MI: Eerdmans, 1996.

Hayward, John. "Revival or Extinction? An Application of Systems Dynamics to Church Attendance and Membership Data." *Church Growth Modeling*, 2002, https://churchmodel.org.uk.

Hiebert, Paul. "Conversion, Culture and Cognitive Categories." *Persona*, 21 June 2010, https://danutm.wordpress.com/2010/06/25/conversion-culture-and-cognitive-categories-4/hiebert-paul-g-conversion-culture-and-cognitive-categories.

Lifeway. "Authority, Authoritarianism, and the Millennial Generation." *Lifeway Leadership*, 26 Sept. 2018, https://leadership.lifeway.com/2015/02/19/authority-authoritarianism-and-the-millennial-generation.

Lipka, Michael. "A Closer Look at America's Rapidly Growing Religious 'Nones'." *Pew Research Center*, 27 July 2020, https://www.pewresearch.org/fact-tank/2015/05/13/a-closer-look-at-americas-rapidly-growing-religious-nones/

Mancini, Will. *Church Unique: How Missional Leaders Cast Vision, Capture Culture, and Create Movement*. San Francisco, Jossey-Bass, 2008.

Mattingly, Terry. "Surviving 2020: How Many Churches Will Die Because of Covid-19 and 'Worship Shifting'?" *GetReligion*, 20 Sept. 2020, https://www.getreligion.org/getreligion/2020/9/16/surviving-2020-how-many-churches-will-die-because-of-covid-19-and-worship-shifting.

Nonprofit Source. "Church and Religious Charitable Giving Statistics. https://nonprofitssource.com/online-giving-statistics/, 2018.

Rainer, Thom S. *The Post-Quarantine Church: Six Urgent Challenges + Opportunities That Will Determine the Future of Your Congregation*. Carol Stream, IL: Tyndale, 2020.

Roba, Tomáš. "Millennials and Generation Z Most Skeptical. They Have No Trust in Social Media and Fear Climate Change." *HST*, Deloitte, 2020, https://www.hst.cz/en/news/blog/1904-millennials-and-generation-z-most-sceptical-they-have-no-trust-in-social-media-and-fear-climate-change.

Rohrmayer, Gary. "Six Causes for Evangelistic Entropy." *Your Journey Blog with Gary Rohrmayer*, 2007, https://garyrohrmayer.typepad.com/yourjourneyblog/2007/10/six-reasons-for.html.

Rohrmayer, Gary. "The Spiritual Journey Guide." *Gary Rohrmayer*, 2 May 2015, https://garyrohrmayer.wordpress.com/spiritual-journey-guide-by-gary-rohrmayer/

Ross, Bobby. "102,000 Fewer People in the Pews since '03: Churches of Christ in Decline." *The Christian Chronicle*, 7 Feb. 2012, https://christianchronicle.org/102-000-fewer-people-in-the-pews-since-03-churches-of-christ-in-decline.

Rushford, Jerry. *Christians on the Oregon Trail: Churches of Christ and Christian Churches in Early Oregon, 1842-1882*. College Press, 1997.

Royster, Carl H. Churches of Christ in the United State 2018. Nashville, TN: 21st Century Christian, 2018.

Shimron, Yonat. "Attendance Hemorrhaging at Small and Midsize US Congregations." *Religion News Service*, 15 Oct. 2021, https://religionnews.com/2021/10/14/study-attendance-at-small-and-midsize-us-congregations-is-hemorrhaging.

Siebert, Jimmy. *Disciple Makers Handbook*. Antioch Community Church, January 2018, https://antioch.org/wp-content/uploads/2018/01/Disciple-Makers-Handbook.pdf.

Siegler, MG. "Eric Schmidt: Every 2 Days We Create as Much Information as We Did up to 2003." *TechCrunch*, 4 Aug. 2010, https://techcrunch.com/2010/08/04/schmidt-data.

Sjogren, Steve. *Conspiracy of Kindness: A Unique Approach to Sharing the Love of Jesus*. Bethany House, 2014.

Sjogren, Steve. "94 Servant Evangelism Ideas for Your Church." *Steve Sjogren Blog*, 25 July 2020, https://www.stevesjogren.com/94-servant-evangelism-ideas-for-your-church.

Smith, Gregory A. "In U.S., Decline of Christianity Continues at Rapid Pace." *Pew Research Center's Religion & Public Life Project*, Pew Research Center, 9 June 2020, https://www.pewforum.org/2019/10/17/in-u-s-decline-of-christianity-continues-at-rapid-pace.

Statista Research Department. "Church Attendance of Americans 2020." *Statista*, Statista Research Department, 15 Jan. 2021, https://www.statista.com/statistics/245491/church-attendance-of-americans/.

Stetzer, Ed. "If It Doesn't Stem Its Decline, Mainline Protestantism Has Just 23 Easters Left." *The Washington Post*, WP Company, 28 April 2017, https://www.washingtonpost.com/news/acts-of-faith/wp/2017/04/28/if-it-doesnt-stem-its-decline-mainline-protestantism-has-just-23-easters-left.

Tippens, Darryl L. *Pilgrim Heart: The Way of Jesus in Everyday Life*. Abilene, TX: Leafwood Publishers, 2006.

White, James Emory. *The Rise of the Nones: Understanding and Reaching the Religiously Unaffiliate*d. Grand Rapids, MI: Baker, 2014.

ABOUT THE AUTHOR

Dr. Stanley E. Granberg serves on the Heritage 21 board and is a founding member of the Heritage 21 Foundation. He served for fifteen years as the director of Kairos Church Planting, a ministry that recruits, trains, and supports church planting leaders across the United States.

Stan was born in Seattle, Washington and raised in the fellowship of the Churches of Christ. He attended Harding University (BS 1978), Harding Graduate School of Religion (MTh 1983), Fuller Theological Seminary (ThM 1996) and the Open University/Oxford Centre for Mission Studies (PhD 2000). He is a trained StratOp and Life Plan facilitator through the Paterson Center and a CoachNet trained coach.

Stan has worked in a variety of ministry roles:

- Youth minister for the East Frayser Church of Christ, Memphis, TN, 1979-1983
- Missionary church planter and leadership trainer among the Meru people of central Kenya, 1983-1993
- Missionary-in-Residence at Lubbock Christian University, Lubbock, TX, 1993-1996
- Bible faculty at Cascade College, Portland, OR, 1996-2004
- Founding director of Kairos Church Planting, 2005-2019
- Executive minister for the Southwest Church of Christ, Jonesboro, AR, 2020-2021

Dr. Granberg's publications include:

- "A Case Study of Growth and Decline: The Churches of Christ, 2006-2016." *Great Commission Research Journal, 10*(1), 90-113, 2018.

- *Spiritual Formation: The Foundation*. Amazon: Create Space, 2015.

- *Leading Others: Sharing.* Amazon: Create Space, 2015.

- *100 Years of African Missions*: *Essays in Honor of Wendell Broom.* Abilene, TX: ACU Press, 2001.

He and his wife, Gena, partnered in ministry as missionaries in Meru, Kenya (1983-1993) and in church planting through Kairos Church Planting. They have four adult children who serve God's kingdom as ministers, church planters, missionaries, and church leaders.

The Granbergs currently live in the Seattle, Washington metro region where they are watching the future of the American church form.

Made in the USA
Coppell, TX
26 June 2024